IT'S TOTALLY NORMAL!

of related interest

How to Understand Your Gender
A practical guide for exploring who you are
Alex Iantaffi and Meg-John Barker
Foreword by S. Bear Bergman
ISBN 978 1 78592 746 1
eISBN 978 1 78450 517 2

They/Them/Their
A Guide to Nonbinary and Genderqueer Identities
Eris Young
ISBN 978 1 78592 483 5
eISBN 978 1 78450 872 2

The Gender Friend
A 102 Guide to Gender Identity
Oakley Phoenix
Foreword by Jackson Bird
ISBN 978 1 83997 357 4
eISBN 978 1 83997 358 1

Queer Sex
A Trans and Non-Binary Guide to Intimacy,
Pleasure and Relationships
Juno Roche
ISBN 978 1 78592 406 4
eISBN 978 1 78450 770 1

It's
TOTALLY
NORMAL!

An LGBTQIA+ Guide to
Puberty, Sex, and Gender

Monica Gupta Mehta
& Asha Lily Mehta

Illustrated by Fox Fisher

Jessica Kingsley Publishers
London and Philadelphia

First published in Great Britain in 2023 by Jessica Kingsley Publishers
An imprint of John Murray Press

I

Disclaimer: The information contained in this book is not intended to replace the
services of trained medical professionals or to be a substitute for medical advice.
You are advised to consult a doctor on any matters relating to your health, and in
particular on any matters that may require diagnosis or medical attention.

A CIP catalogue record for this title is available from the
British Library and the Library of Congress

ISBN 978 1 83997 355 0
eISBN 978 1 83997 356 7

Printed and bound in the United States by Integrated Books International

Jessica Kingsley Publishers' policy is to use papers that are natural, renewable
and recyclable products and made from wood grown in sustainable forests.
The logging and manufacturing processes are expected to conform to the
environmental regulations of the country of origin.

Jessica Kingsley Publishers
Carmelite House
50 Victoria Embankment
London EC4Y 0DZ

www.jkp.com

John Murray Press
Part of Hodder & Stoughton Limited
An Hachette UK Company

To our kin,
because family is what we make it

Contents

Introduction

i, I'm Monica—mother, teacher, educational psychologist, and now "author"!

My teen Asha and I run a nonprofit called Normalizers, which provides education and support for LGBTQIA and autistic youth. We started an anonymous sex ed question box and opened it up to teenagers from all around the world. We hoped to answer all your questions through our TikTok (@monicatheteacher) and podcast (The Normalizers). Eventually, after hundreds of questions piled up, we joked that we'd need an entire book to answer them all. And so here we are!

Luckily, we're not easily embarrassed. In this book, we have answered all of your questions (almost a thousand in total!)—about masturbation, pornography, fetishes, and anything else that came our way. Some of my personal favorites were: "Is it awkward???" and "How do I know which is the right hole?" We have included a Q&A at the end of each chapter to answer some of your questions directly.

Even the basic question of "What is sex?" needed to be answered in a more inclusive way than usual. Defining sex as "penis-in-vagina intercourse" ignores so many other forms of sex, and the majority of the LGBTQIA+ community.

Most school sex ed programs are not LGBTQIA+ inclusive enough to answer these types of questions. They are also not honest, realistic, or taught with a sense of humor. Because let's face it—sex is (often) funny!

In this book, we'll start with an overview of puberty, in all its awkward glory. Next, we'll jump right in to all of your questions about sex, including how you even "do it." We've devoted a chapter to consent, although we could write an entire book about this topic and still not cover it fully.

We discuss how to have safer sex and what to do if you end up not being safe. We've done our best to help you understand the wide world of sexuality and gender. The book concludes with some social-emotional learning about relationships and societal expectations. Most of the SEL and basic sex ed content was written by me and edited by Asha to be more teen focused and relatable.

You'll also find little asides throughout the book, personal stories from around the world. Sometimes hearing someone's own story is more powerful than a thousand explanations. Asha has gathered these anonymous anecdotes from our various social media communities, which are indicated with a ♥. Sometimes I have included my own stories, which are indicated with a ★ throughout.

We hope you find this book helpful, informative, and fun!

Much love,
Monica (she/her) and
Asha (they/them)

Note: There are some terms we use in this book that will be new to most people but important to understand. Words that might be new have been introduced first in bold, indicating that they are also defined in the glossary. One important such set of terms is AMAB and AFAB. AMAB is a term for someone who was born with what are considered to be "male" body parts (specifically a penis), and therefore is "assigned male at birth." I use this terminology because it is transgender and intersex inclusive — it acknowledges that people may be assumed to be a gender that is not who they really are. The term AFAB means "assigned female at birth" and describes someone born with a vagina. Intersex will be explained more later, but some people are not AMAB or AFAB because their biological sex is not clearly aligned with male or female.

Chapter 1

"I Love Puberty!"
(Said No One, Ever)

et's face it—puberty has a bad rep. Puberty means random erections, body odor, bleeding out of your vagina, sore breasts, and acne. But puberty also means the excitement of crushes, identity exploration, and exploring physical intimacy. It's a roller coaster, but at least it's one we all ride together.

Puberty is the time when your body and your brain transition from childhood to adulthood. These changes usually start between ages 8 and 14, and they occur in gradual stages until about 14 to 16 years old. People with **vaginas** often go through puberty earlier than those with **penises**. Yes, I could have said **females** go through puberty earlier than **males**...but throughout this book I will be normalizing the experience of the **transgender (trans)** community.

Puberty can be confusing and stressful, which is why it is good to find a trusted adult to talk with. But sometimes we have questions we are too embarrassed to ask in person. And the internet is full of untrustworthy answers. I asked tweens and teens to send in the questions they were too shy to ask out loud. Most of this book will be my answers to those questions.

Help! I can't stop smiling!

As you go through puberty, you'll likely feel **romantic** and/or sexual attraction to others. I had my first real crush at age 11... to the person I'm still happily married to at 42 (**demisexual things**, ha!). But that is *not* the norm! You'll likely have many crushes in your life, starting as early as elementary school. It's more common to start experiencing sexual attraction in middle school. Some people are **asexual**, meaning they don't feel "typical" sexual attraction. This does *not* necessarily mean they don't have **sex**, which I will explain more in the chapter about sexuality.

It feels good to have a crush—your brain releases dopamine, a "feel-good" hormone. People often feel giddy or excited when they see their crush, as well as anxious to act perfectly around them. Because it feels so good to your brain to think of your crush, you might find yourself thinking of them often, even obsessively. I have hundreds of notes I wrote to my friends about Nick (my husband) from all throughout middle school.

The reason we start feeling this attraction to others is mostly biological—attraction to others and feeling super "horny" is what helps create babies to continue the species. However, some of how we feel is also linked to social norms. We get messages from watching people around us, from social media, TV, movies, and music. Many of these messages encourage teens to focus on relationships. These messages are often **heteronormative**, meaning they focus on **heterosexual** relationships, so much so that other forms of attraction feel taboo or wrong. People who are gay might find themselves attracted to someone of the opposite **gender** simply because they believe that's what they *should* feel. People who are asexual might find themselves forming crushes just to fit in with their friends and peers.

It's completely natural to have crushes that come and go, and to want to be in a relationship. It's also okay not to be as focused on that part of your life, or not to feel those same emotions. If you do end up in a relationship, be sure only to do what you feel comfortable with physically and emotionally. While it's natural to be a little anxious about firsts, like a first kiss, if you feel pressured physically, it's always okay to stop at any time.

★ My first kiss was not until I was 17. I was visiting my brother in college, and my boyfriend flew in to surprise me. We went on our first real date (I wasn't allowed to date at the time, so we had never been out anywhere just the two of us). I remember Nick (my husband now) kissed me on my brother's porch as we headed out. We were both so awkward. We kept bumping noses because both of us have big noses. But that memory is something I love now. Your first kiss doesn't have to be perfect. If it's with the right person, it will be perfect however it goes. And if it's not the right person, I hope you have a great first kiss when you are with the right person, and that's the story you can tell when you are as old as me.

What's that smell?...and other changes

During puberty, you will start to sweat more, and you might develop stronger body odor. I refused to set foot in one of my kids' rooms for about a week one time because they weren't showering daily and had run out of deodorant. I recommend using a "name brand" deodorant and testing it out to make sure it suits your skin—if you have sensitive skin, it might take a few tries to find one that suits you.

There are lots of other changes you can expect as well. These include:

Acne

Why is something that is so common still so embarrassing? Pimples (or "zits") are perfectly normal, and most people find they can manage them through a simple routine of keeping their face clean and applying gentle acne products. A lot of people overuse acne products and their face dries out, which creates a cycle of more acne. Some simple lifestyle changes can also help manage it—cleaning your phone, drinking plenty of water, avoiding too much sugar, and keeping your sheets and towels clean. Do *not* squeeze, pop, or otherwise mess with your pimples, or you'll risk creating an infection or spreading the acne.

If your acne is bothering you, you can ask a doctor for their advice. If you have constant acne rashes, your acne is painful, you are getting scarring, or your face is getting overly dry or oily, these are all things a dermatologist can help you with.

Hair
So much new hair. You'll start growing hair under your armpits, around your genitals (pubic hair), and possibly more on your arms and legs. Your hair might also get darker. For **AMAB** people (those assigned male at birth), you might start growing hair on your face, chest, and back as well. AFABs (those assigned female at birth) might also experience hair growth here, but typically less than AMABs do. I'll discuss how to manage your new hair growth more below.

Growing pains
You might notice some occasional pain in your arms and legs as you grow. This is normal, but again, if it's too bothersome, talk to your doctor.

Voice changes
AMABs have a bump in their throat called an Adam's apple (or

laryngeal prominence), which might get larger. AMAB voices typically get lower and deeper during puberty, while AFAB voices also deepen a bit, but it is much less noticeable than AMAB voices. If your voice cracks as it changes, that's totally normal, and the cracking should go away in time.

Anatomy
Your genitals will likely grow larger. This includes AMAB penises and testicles, and AFAB labia (the folds of skin on the outside of the vagina). AFAB **breasts** grow larger during puberty, and hips widen. AMAB chests and shoulders often broaden.

Menstruation
If you have a uterus, your **period** will likely start at this time. During your period, blood from your uterus leaves through your vagina. This usually happens about once a month for a few days each cycle. Let your doctor know if your period hasn't started by 15 years old (or three years after you start having your first puberty changes). A lot of questions in our anonymous sex ed question box have to do with menstruation, so I've included a much larger section about periods later in this chapter.

Emotions
As your hormones change, you are likely to feel more emotional. You may experience mood swings, or find your emotions are more intense. It's a good idea to find healthy outlets for your emotions, as well as people who you can talk to. This could be family members, friends, friends' parents, online communities, teachers, school counselors, or anyone you trust to be supportive and caring.

If you find that your emotions are interfering negatively

with your life, more than seems normal, you should talk to your doctor about it. Sometimes people go through a period of depression, anger, or anxiety that is beyond just normal "mood swings." If you think this sounds like you, don't let others convince you that it will just pass on its own. There is help out there, in the form of medication and/or therapy, to help you feel better.

Stress
Puberty is often a time of increased stress and anxiety. It can help to have regular physical exercise to combat this. It's also great to have creative outlets for your emotions and stress, such as writing, art, theater, and/or music.

Sexual thoughts
You might notice you have sexual thoughts, urges, dreams, and/or fantasies. You might feel suddenly aroused at unexpected times, including first thing in the morning. Slang for this would be feeling "horny," "in the mood," or "turned on." We'll talk a lot more about **masturbation** and sex throughout the book.

Size doesn't matter...AMAB, AFAB, and intersex anatomy

You likely have some combination of breasts, vulva, penis, testicles, and/or anus (sometimes referred to as *butt*). AMABs have a penis, testicles, and an anus. AFABs have breasts, a vulva (the outside of the vagina), and an anus. **Intersex** people are sometimes born with a combination of "male" and "female" genitalia, but not always.

Up until now, I have been referring to the "vagina" because

it is the term most people use when talking about their vulva (well, that or something slang like *vag* or *pussy*). The vulva is the correct name for the outside visible part of your genitals (if you have a vagina). This includes your labia (the lips), clitoris, vaginal opening, and the opening to your urethra, where you pee out of. The vagina is actually the inside part, a very stretchy organ that connects your vulva to your uterus.

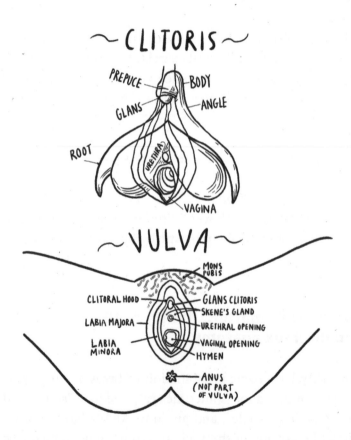

One of the most misunderstood parts of AFAB anatomy is the hymen. The hymen is a thin tissue covering the vaginal opening. I was taught that the hymen covers the full opening and tears the first time you have sex. This is not exactly true. Some people's hymens do cover most of their vagina. But some people have barely any hymen tissue at all. Your hymen can thin out from all kinds of everyday activities, such as sports, biking, horseback riding, masturbating, or using tampons, as you grow. A gynecologist cannot tell if you've had sex by studying your hymen. Some scientists think the hymen helps keep your vagina clean of bacteria when you are younger; as you get older, you will develop pubic hair that can also serve this purpose.

A lot of teens want to know if their sexual anatomy is normal. They want to know if their breasts are big or small, if their nipples are weird, or how their penis compares to others.

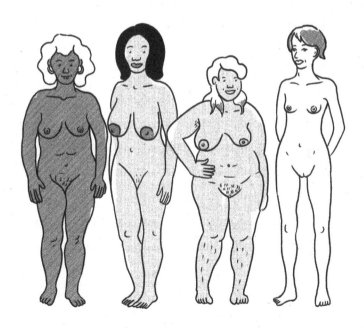

When it comes to breasts, almost anything is normal. Breasts can range from small to big, be uneven, and come in all shapes and colors. Breasts change over your lifetime, with the most change occurring between ages 8 and 14 (during puberty). Losing and gaining weight, pregnancy, breastfeeding, and age all affect their shape and size. When your body changes and stretches, it can form stretch marks. These are really common and often fade over time. You should be familiar with the feel and look of your breasts, and let a doctor know right away if you notice a change, such as a lump.

Whatever size breasts you develop is natural for you. People spend a lot of time and energy trying to make their breasts larger, sometimes in unsafe ways. Please be aware that the images that you see in the media represent a societal ideal that really only matches a handful of bodies. Some people do have medical reasons for performing surgery on their breasts; for example, breast reduction surgery can be beneficial in reducing back pain.

A lot of people worry about the size and shape of their nipples as well. Nipples and the areola (the darker circle around your nipple) can be all different colors, from pink to dark brown to black. Some nipples are inverted, or go inwards, and some are flat or stick out a bit. It's normal for your nipples to get hard when aroused (turned on). It's also normal for them to get hard in response to touch or cold.

Just like with breasts, a lot of people worry about their penis size and shape. Penises also vary a lot—some are bigger or smaller, some have a little curve or bend to them. All of this is perfectly normal; the only thing to be concerned about is if your penis hurts, in which case talk to your doctor. Just like with breasts, penises grow during puberty. They also grow larger when erect.

Some people have circumcised penises, which means that the foreskin is removed, and others are uncircumcised. Either way is normal and it doesn't change how your penis works. The only difference to note is that people with uncircumcised penises should pull back the foreskin when washing.

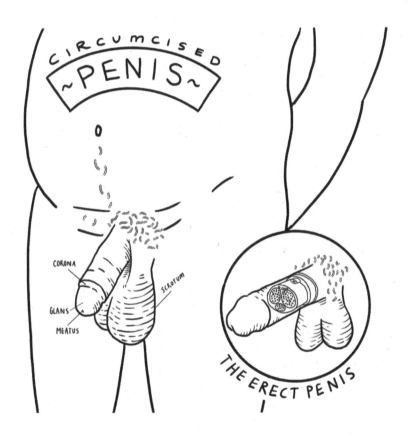

Testicles (slang: *balls*) also come in all different sizes and may be uneven. This is where the sperm is stored and where your body makes testosterone. The scrotum, sitting right near the testicles, keeps the sperm at the right temperature by hanging closer or further away from the body depending on the surrounding temperature. This is why everything might appear to shrink up when exiting a cold pool; this is your body's way of keeping your sperm warm.

One of the most commonly asked questions about penises is whether bigger is really better for sex. The short answer is no. People spend hundreds of dollars on products to enlarge their penises, including creams, pills, and even devices. Most of these do not work, are costly, and can be unsafe. I always tell people it's not about size—it's about learning how to create pleasure during sex. Most people with vaginas don't **orgasm** from deeper penetration—it is typically from some sort of stimulation of the genitals in other ways. For example, it's much more important for vaginal pleasure to know how to stimulate the clitoris than to have a large penis.

Hair, hair, everywhere

During puberty, you are likely to grow new hair in many places of your body. For all sexes, it is natural to grow hair under your armpits, around your genitals, and on your arms and legs. AMABs grow more hair on their face, chest, and back than AFABs do.

People often choose to remove hair from certain areas, most commonly through shaving and/or waxing (though there are other alternatives like creams, lasers, and bleaching the hair rather than removing it). You are not required to remove your hair, ever. Hair growth is perfectly natural, and if it doesn't bother you, you are more than welcome just to leave it exactly as is.

♥ As an Indian girl growing up in America, I felt totally embarrassed by my dark upper lip hair, and I was often teased about my "mustache." I wish my parents had understood my desire to remove some of my hair to fit in with my peers, but even more I wish I'd had the confidence back then just not to care what others thought about me on such a superficial level. I remember in seventh grade I finally got so embarrassed about my hair (most notably in the locker rooms before and after PE) that I snuck a razor and shaved even though I didn't quite know how. I finished with one arm before my mom caught me; luckily, she did let me finish the other arm. She realized I was not going to back down, so ultimately she let me start shaving.

If you do shave, be sure to follow basic safety protocols. Use shaving cream to reduce skin irritation, and do not let your razor blades get dull. Razor blades should ideally be replaced every five to ten shaves. Always wet your skin before shaving; after a shower is an excellent time to shave. When you shave, shave in the direction of hair growth. If you want to stay clean shaven, you will likely need to shave every one to three days. Shaving is less ideal for upper lip hair on females because it can create a thicker stubble. Many people wax their upper lip, or do something called "threading," in which thread is used to rapidly pluck unwanted facial hair.

Cuts or nicks are common when shaving. They shouldn't happen every time; if they are happening often, you might be using a dull blade or not be using enough shaving cream. If you do get a small nick, use a tissue to apply pressure to stop the bleeding. If you have pimples or cuts where you are going to shave, avoid shaving for a few days, or try using an electric razor, which doesn't shave as close to the skin.

Waxing works by pulling hairs out from the roots. This means that a wax will last longer than a shave, typically at least three weeks. There are both soft and hard waxes. If you wax regularly, you may find your hair grows back less and less over time. People who wax often get this done by a professional, though you can learn to do it on your own at home for less sensitive areas (this is *not* recommended to do on your own for pubic hair). If you wax at home, be careful to avoid burns. If you go to a salon for waxing, be sure they use high-quality wax that won't create rashes or irritation on your skin and that they keep everything clean and hygienic.

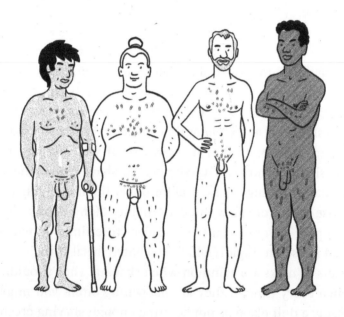

People sometimes choose to trim or remove their pubic hair. Again, this is not required or necessary. But if you want to, you can trim, shave, and/or wax the hair around your genitals. Some trimmers have guards that prevent you from getting too close to your actual skin. If you want to shave, you should first trim the pubic hairs until they are short. Use a fragrance-free shaving cream, pull your skin taut (tight and smooth), and then shave in the direction of your hair growth. It is especially important to make sure your razor blade is sharp for shaving this area. Make sure you can fully see what you are doing to avoid nicking the skin.

It is okay to have any amount of hair around your sexual anatomy—from none at all to your full, natural amount. The hair there actually serves a purpose; it both protects you from debris and bacteria getting into your genitals, and it can reduce unwanted friction during sex.

That time of the month (anyone have a tampon?)

There are so many slang terms for menstruation, or your period. "Code red," "on the rag," "monthly visitor," "time of the month," "surfing the crimson wave/tide"—most of these exist because so many people find it embarrassing to admit they are on their period. I hope we can eventually remove the stigma of using that word, for people of all genders. A period is a natural biological function, and we're long past the days when people would have to hide in caves because they were "unclean" during their periods.

I'm going to write this section not assuming gender, as transgender men may still experience their periods. I saw a photo recently of a men's bathroom stocked with period supplies, and it made my day. I hope we can eventually be that accepting as a general rule in our society.

People typically start having their period during puberty,

around 12–15 years of age. As I said, talk to your doctor if your period has not started by age 15. Periods are not always regular, especially at first, but most people experience their periods in cycles of 21–35 days. The average is a 28-day cycle between period start dates, with average bleeding for two to seven days. There are many apps, such as Flo and Clue, that you can use to track your periods, which can help you predict the start date of your next cycle. If you miss a period and have had penis-in-vagina sex, it is a good idea to do a pregnancy test, even if you used **contraceptives** (protection).

Your period is caused by hormones in your body that help prepare the body for pregnancy. Over the month, the lining of your uterus builds to create a womb for an embryo to implant itself. During ovulation, your ovaries release an egg that can be fertilized by sperm. If you don't get pregnant, the extra uterine lining comes out through your vagina. This period "blood" is actually endometrial tissue, blood, cervical mucus, and vaginal secretions. It's normal for period blood to be red, pink, or brown, and it is also normal for it to not always appear smooth.

★ Just like most people, I learned all about periods in school. I knew that blood would start coming out of my vagina at some point, and that it was a normal part of the reproductive cycle. My mom was really open about periods and period products, so much so that my brother once took a pad and placed it on his teddy bear's bottom as a toddler. So when I woke up one morning with a dark brown stain on my underwear, at age 12, you would think I would have known what was up. Instead, I panicked, fully believing I had pooped my pants. Embarrassed, I threw the underwear away. After a few times of this happening, I didn't know what to do...we were at my cousin's house, and I was out of underwear. I finally brought my mom into the bathroom and showed her what was happening. She laughed so hard, then told me that the dark brown stain was actually dried blood and that I had started my period. It's a really funny story now, but I was completely mortified back then.

There are lots of different ways to catch the blood that comes out during your period. Pads are linings for your underwear that absorb the blood, and they come in all different sizes. Some have wings that wrap around your underwear to keep the pad from bunching up. Tampons are made of absorptive material that can be inserted into your vagina, often using an attached applicator. Tampons come in various sizes, and it might be easier to learn and practice with an extra-small tampon when you first start using them. Many people are nervous about inserting a tampon—remember that the vagina is meant to expand naturally, but it will not do so if you are feeling too anxious or scared. A correctly sized tampon should stay in place securely but not cause any pain. Period underwear is special underwear that has a thicker lining built into it. Menstrual cups are inserted into the vagina to collect the period flow. If you find you have to change your products every hour because they are getting full, you should tell a doctor. On the other hand, if your period is really light, make sure you still change your pad or tampon regularly to avoid irritation.

There are some risks to be aware of when using period products, most notably when using tampons. It is important to always use these products properly. Tampons are regulated by the FDA (Food and Drug Administration) as medical devices because of the risk of toxic shock syndrome, as well as yeast, fungal, and bacterial infections. The FDA has not yet approved any reusable tampons—only single use tampons, and only when changed out at regular time periods (every 4–8 hours). Toxic shock syndrome is caused by certain types of bacteria producing a substance that can cause organ damage. It is very rare, and cases have gone down a lot as people learn how to use tampons safely.

There is lower potential risk, but still some risk, of infection and irritation from other products, such as pads and menstrual cups. Not much research has been done in this area, but pads that are fragrance-free are considered safer by the FDA.

People often keep some form of period supplies in their backpack or bag so they are prepared for a period to start at any time. If yours starts and you don't have supplies, chances are a friend, parent, teacher, or school nurse has them. If you can't find any supplies, it should work to fold up some toilet paper and stick it in your underwear until you can find something better to use.

There are other symptoms people experience with their periods. If you experience painful cramping, there are over-the-counter pain medications that can help, as well as non-medical comforts, such as warm water bottles and/or warm baths. Some people find laying down helps, and others find walking around or stretching relieves some of their cramps. One of my family members was in so much pain from period cramps that she would end up almost passing out on the floor of the bathroom, and one time in the supermarket aisle. If your cramps are that bad, talk to a doctor about medication that can help reduce the severity.

Other **PMS** (**premenstrual syndrome**) symptoms include bloating in your stomach area, acne breakouts, tiredness, and soreness in your breasts. The bloating can sometimes cause temporary weight gain during your period. Some people find that they are extra emotional before their period. Transgender women who are taking hormones can sometimes experience the monthly emotions of a period without the actual blood flow. If any of your PMS symptoms impact your life negatively, it's a good idea to talk with a doctor to see what relief they can offer you.

♥ My PMS was never that bad until I hit 30...then all of a sudden, I was picking fights with everyone for the two days before my period would start, every single month. I was undeservedly harsh and critical, impatient, and very low on warmth and empathy. I don't know who was more relieved when I started taking medication to manage my PMS, me or my family. Eventually as I aged, my hormones changed again, and my PMS improved on its own.

If you do get pregnant, your period will temporarily stop, as the uterine lining will be used to create a womb for the baby. If you have a regular period that is late, it's important to get tested for pregnancy. You can buy pregnancy test kits in most pharmacies, or you can go to a clinic or doctor's office. And yes, you can get pregnant or have sex while on your period... as they say, the only thing a period fully stops is a sentence.

There's no right or wrong way to masturbate

Masturbation is any form of touching yourself to experience sexual pleasure. As embarrassed as people are to talk about their periods, they are often even more embarrassed to talk about masturbation. That doesn't stop them from coming up with over a hundred slang terms for it (yes, that was a pretty hilarious and emotionally scarring Google search). Some of the most common are "jerking off" or "jacking off," "wanking," "rubbing one out," "flickin' the bean," "beating it," and "finger painting." By the time this book gets published, I am sure there will be even newer terms, and even more puns ("*I used to have a masturbation addiction, but luckily I 'beat it.'*")

Masturbation is completely normal and natural. Even young children touch their genitals because it feels enjoyable. But not everyone masturbates, and it is also totally normal to not really enjoy it or want to do it. Unfortunately, there are many cultural and religious stigmas around masturbation. If you have heard of anything bad happening when you masturbate, it is likely not true. You won't go blind from masturbating too much, your penis or clitoris won't fall off, and it won't make sex less enjoyable. If anything, masturbation can help teach you which touches you most enjoy, which is information that can be helpful to share with a partner later.

♥ I never used to really enjoy my partner touching my clitoris. Neither oral sex or with his finger really felt that good. I couldn't figure out what was wrong with my clit—it just felt like I didn't have one. One time when using a vibrator I laid on my side and it suddenly felt SO good. That's how I realized my clit was a bit to the side, and that's why it had never felt as good when my partner would finger me in the center of my vag. I might have gone my whole life without that kind of orgasm if it wasn't for that happy accident.

One common question I get is how to know if you are masturbating too much. There is really no such thing as masturbating too much healthwise, unless it is interfering with your life. If you feel that it is getting in the way of you living a healthy life, talk with your doctor. Some people masturbate daily, some weekly, some once in a while, some not at all. It's totally okay if masturbation doesn't feel pleasurable to you. If it is painful, however, then this is something you should definitely discuss with a doctor.

To be safe when masturbating, make sure anything you use is clean and hygienic. Many people masturbate with only their hands, while some use **sex toys**, such as vibrators, to help stimulate their body. People with penises most often masturbate by stroking their erect penis until they orgasm, after which the penis goes back to being flaccid. Some use a **condom** to make clean up easier, or a tissue to clean up the ejaculate. Some people use **lubricant** (**lube**), which helps reduce friction.

People with vaginas most often masturbate by touching their clitoris, located at the top center of the vulva (the vaginal "lips"). People use their fingers or a vibrator to stimulate the clitoris. Some prefer to use their fingers because they have complete control of speed and intensity, and they like the intimacy of pleasuring their own body. Some prefer a vibrator because it can make a more intense orgasm and because it is "less work." If using your fingers, you can try pulling back the clitoral hood and rubbing the clitoris in a way that feels good to you. You don't have to stick to the clitoris—you might find you really enjoy nipple stimulation and/or vaginal penetration, as well as caresses on other parts of your body. If you decide to use your fingers for penetration, you can locate the "G-spot" inside the vagina by hooking your fingers toward the clitoris. The G-spot is actually the back portion of the clitoris, so this is stimulating the same nerves but internally.

A common form of masturbation involves using visual imagery to help create that feeling of being aroused. These days, a lot of people use the internet to search up pornography, and they can often unintentionally come across images that are too advanced for their maturity level. This is why it's so important for parents to monitor internet usage at a young age, and to teach their tweens and teens how to self-monitor and identify when something is inappropriate for them. While it is perfectly natural to use pornography or sexual images and videos to masturbate, it can be damaging emotionally to come across pornography before you are ready, or pornography that is unhealthily graphic or even violent. Remember that most porn is not a realistic depiction of real-life sex.

★ When my first-born child was only eight or nine, they often searched things up on the internet on their own. One day, they were hanging out with their cousin (same age) in the family room when they decided to look for Harry Potter videos. A simple Google search went wrong, and soon they showed up by my side looking quite concerned. They asked me to come see a video that might have been "bad." I walked in and immediately recognized the sounds of sexual activity. They had completely unintentionally found a video of Harry Potter characters drinking and having sex with one another. I don't know if they even really remember it, but it certainly scarred *me* for life!

So how do you find "safe" porn? Not only do I want to steer you clear of unhealthy depictions of sex and of women, but most porn sites aren't that safe to click on due to viruses or hackers. If you aren't really looking for intense pornography, you might find the sexy scenes on Netflix or sex scenes in a book are all you need to get in the mood. A lot of places offer "smut" to read online, including the infamous Wattpad. There are apps that let you listen to audio porn, such as Dipsea, Ferly, and Quinn, which many people enjoy even more than visual pornography, as it leaves the images up to your imagination. If you are looking for something with more intense video porn, there is a site called Bellesa that was created for and by women. There is also Indie Porn Revolution, which contains both straight and queer porn, and there is the Crash Pad Series. Some people might prefer Make Love Not Porn, which aims to showcase more of what sex actually looks like in real life, which is very different than what you find on most porn sites.

Be careful if you search up porn sites, because you will find extremely graphic images and videos right on the homepage. Do *not* feel pressured to look at porn sites that are as intense as these ones...a lot of people find them uncomfortable, cheesy, unrealistic, or even a total turn-off. But for those who enjoy porn, it is often the audio (the sounds of moaning) and the sexy stories that turn them on.

Erections

What human body part is long, hard, bendable, most useful when erect, and contains the letters p, e, n, i, and s?

Your spine, silly.

An **erection** is the hardening of the penis, which causes it to enlarge and point away from the body. Erections are often called "boners," "wood," or "stiffies." Erections happen from infancy (they can even happen in the womb!), but it is not until puberty that erections happen due to being turned on. Because of an increase in hormones, they start happening a lot more often, and they can often happen when not in a sexual situation. Erections happen when extra blood flows into the penis and creates pressure, making the penis expand and harden.

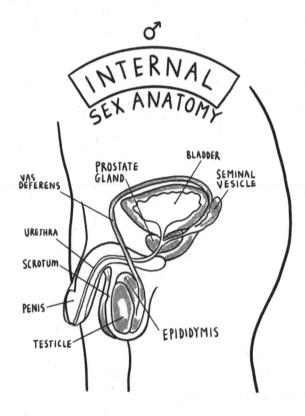

Many people find their early erections embarrassing, especially when they happen at awkward moments. If you are caught off guard by an erection, there are things you can do to ease the embarrassment. If you can think of a reason to sit down, you can hide your erection between your legs. If you are standing, you could find a way to cover it, such as by using a book or a jacket. Someone told me that they bend over to pretend to tie their shoe if caught totally by surprise. If you need to, you could always say you need to use the restroom to exit the situation.

♥ When I first realized it felt really good to rub my boner against things, I was still pretty young. I knew it felt good so I did it, without really thinking about it. Well eventually, one of those times, I orgasmed, and I had no idea what happened. It felt good but also really alarming, and suddenly there was like wet stuff and my penis wasn't stiff and I just really thought I broke it. I literally went and woke up my mom. I felt so dumb later when I realized what had happened, and my mom sometimes still laughs about it.

Ejaculation, or "cumming," happens if you masturbate or have sex until orgasm. An erection will also just go away on its own if you wait it out. During ejaculation, semen (containing sperm) comes out through the tip of the penis. This fluid is different from urine (pee). It is not possible to pee when ejaculating. After ejaculation, the hardness in the penis will go away.

Often, people ejaculate in their sleep, the AMAB version of having a "wet dream." If you wake up with an erection, people often refer to that as "morning wood." It can make it more difficult to pee until the erection subsides.

Identity exploration

A normal and natural part of puberty is exploring identity labels surrounding gender and sexuality. We often try on all kinds of labels—being emo, athletic, academic, artistic, or leaning in to our ethnic backgrounds. Just as you might think you are totally into theater and end up instead loving basketball, you might not understand your true gender or sexual identity until you explore it further. That's totally okay. Your teenage years are a great time to figure out who you are, in all ways.

The majority of people in the world identify as heterosexual, or "straight," and cisgender. Heterosexual means that you feel sexual and/or romantic attraction to the opposite gender. For example, if you are a girl who is attracted only to boys, that would be heterosexual. **Cisgender** means you identify as the gender that you were assumed to be at birth. So if you were born with a penis and declared a boy, a cisgender person would still identify as a boy as they grow.

There are *many* other gender and sexuality terms, often collectively referred to as the LGBTQIA+, LGBTQ+, LGBT, or the queer community. Since these identities are underrepresented in media, and considered taboo in various communities, people who aren't cisgender and straight often find themselves confused about their sexuality and/or gender. Those who are in the majority are often much more confident in their identities, as they are exposed to plenty of representation that matches how they feel. This is called **heteronormativity**—the idea that our culture normalizes heterosexuality only. While it is true that the majority of people are heterosexual, our culture often treats heterosexuality as the *preferred* sexuality, or worse, as the only acceptable one.

Cisnormativity: the same concept except about being cisgender (the same gender as you were assumed at birth based on your genitals). As we grow up we learn many gendered stereotypes and expectations; as a young transgender child it can be quite confusing to not identify with the role you have been assigned. Yet the majority of transgender kids are expected to go along with these roles until they are old enough to question them. This leads to not only a lot of confusion about gender, but also a higher degree of mental health struggles in the transgender community.

Comphet: another often-quoted term, short for "compulsory heterosexuality." Lesbians use comphet to explain their early crushes on boys that later disappear. The term means that they were so exposed to heterosexuality as the only way to be that their brain formed crushes that were not natural to their orientation.

Compallo: a similar term, but is short for "compulsory allosexuality."

Allosexuality: just a fancy word for someone who feels sexual attraction—the opposite of asexuality. Many asexuals are so exposed to the idea that it is "normal" to feel sexual attraction that their brain forms these feelings, but they aren't legitimate desires or emotions. As an asexual individual myself, I can say it was very confusing not experiencing crushes or physical touch in the same way as my friends. Many people assume asexuality means not having sex at all, but there are actually many different forms of asexuality, some of which include a desire for sex.

Later, I will go into more detail about the LGBTQIA+ community. For now, I will simply encourage you to be open to understanding your own identity and to be a strong ally to your queer peers and friends.

Visiting the doctor

As you go through puberty, you will likely have annual wellness visits with the doctor. At some of these, you will receive vaccinations to protect you against STIs (**sexually transmitted infections**) in the future. Your doctor will routinely check private areas to make sure you are developing as you should. It is important to know that no adult should *ever* touch these areas without your permission, as well as consent from your parents or legal guardians.

Other than routine visits, it is a good idea to visit the doctor if you are thinking about being sexually active. This doesn't mean only penis-in-vagina sex—this includes **oral sex** as well as any other sexual activity involving the genitals, including "hand jobs" and "fingering." The doctor can help you obtain protection as well as STI testing. If you have any new lumps, pain, itching, bumps, burning, or any other changes to your breasts or genitals, you should visit the doctor to have them evaluated as soon as possible.

Your doctor or gynecologist can also help you obtain **birth control** contraceptives. These help you reduce the risk of pregnancy. There is more on safer sex later in the book.

Anonymous sex ed question box

"Can you have sex on your period?"

Absolutely. But make sure you and your partner are both okay with it. Not everyone is, and that's fine. If you do have sex during your period, you might want to use a towel or something you don't mind staining underneath you. Make sure you do *not* have a tampon in! And remember, you *can* get pregnant on your period.

"Will having sex during my period change my cycle?"

There's not much evidence to answer this question well. There are reports of uterine contractions shortening the length of a period, or of hormone changes delaying your period. But nothing I have read has enough evidence to say that having sex directly impacts your cycle.

"How do I tell my mom I want to use tampons instead of pads?"

There are a number of reasons people might prefer tampons, and there are some reasons parents are against them. If you want to use tampons so you can go swimming on your period, it might help to let your mom know that you will use pads or period underwear at other times, which will reduce any risk from using tampons. You should also understand how to use tampons safely, and let your mom know that you have researched how to do this. You need to change tampons frequently and wash your hands each time you are removing or placing one.

If your mom is worried about TSS (toxic shock syndrome), it could be helpful to discuss the improvements in tampons since her childhood, and to let her know that you know how to prevent TSS. TSS is very rare but very serious, so it is important to follow basic safety protocols. Wash your hands really well, use the lowest absorbency tampon that works for you, try to use other products when you don't *need* the tampon, and be sure to change your tampon very frequently. Realizing you know how to properly use tampons might help reassure your mom.

"How do you tell your parents you got your first period?"

If one of your parents has a uterus, they likely have been through a similar set of emotions. They have also likely had their period for decades and view it as a totally normal and natural part of life. Remember that while it is probably a very big change in your life, it is normal to them. Just be straight-forward about the fact that yours has started and that you need some hygiene products. If you don't have a parent who has personal experience with periods, they will likely still know enough people to not find the concept embarrassing. And if you don't feel comfortable talking directly to them, you can always talk to a different trusted adult and perhaps that person can help you inform your parents.

"Is it okay to have wet dreams of girls even though I'm a straight female?"

Only you can decide your sexuality, but if you are having sexual fantasies about girls that are making you orgasm, it is possible you are not straight. But yes, it is okay to have wet dreams about your sexual fantasies. And yes, people with vaginas have wet dreams too, though they are often less obvious than waking up to ejaculation in your sheets. You may find your vagina is extra lubricated when you awake, or that your underwear has some clear discharge.

"How do girls masturbate?"

All people masturbate the same way—essentially by figuring
out which parts of their body feel good to touch and touching
those parts. This is usually done in private and when relaxed.
Some people use pornography or other visual things to help
them get "in the mood." For people with vaginas and breasts,
it is usually a combination of rubbing the clitoris, inserting
a finger or two into the vagina to simulate penetration, and
touching one's nipples.

"I can't find the clit. I know where it's supposed to be, but there's no feeling when I try to find it."

Some people have a smaller clitoris and larger hood over
the top, which can make it tricky to find the clitoris. I know
you said you know where it is located, but be sure you are
looking in the right spot. Many people think it is closer to
the vagina than it actually is. The clitoris is located at the
very top of where the labia ("lips") meet, under a protective
skin hood. Some people find they can see it better by using
a mirror to understand their anatomy. Some people find it
by starting at the base of the vaginal opening and using
their fingers to gently pull back the flaps of the labia until
they reach the top, checking for a small bump or stronger
sensation along the way.

If you really can't find it, there is no shame in asking your
gynecologist or doctor to check for it at your next visit. It
might be embarrassing for some people, but keep in mind
they hear things like that every day. And it is possible for
the clitoris to be slightly off center, or for the clitoral hood
to not be retracting properly.

"Where does the sperm come out of?"

Sperm comes out in fluid known as semen. It comes out the urethra, the same hole in which a person with a penis pees from. There is a mechanism inside that stops pee from coming out when sexually aroused.

"What can I do to make my vaginal area smell nice?"

Your vagina really ought to just smell like a healthy vagina. Many people report that the smell of the vagina is a major turn-on for them. There are many products sold to deodorize, douche, or fragrance the vagina, but these can be harmful to your natural body chemistry. It *is* important to keep your vagina clean, but you should do this simply by using mild soap and water in the shower, not by inserting things into your vagina (you don't need to—discharge is your vagina's way of cleaning itself!). Make sure you wear clean underwear each day.

Pay attention to your diet. Certain foods can cause a change in your vaginal odor. Some of the most common ones include spices, onion, broccoli, garlic, smoked foods, asparagus, meat (in large quantities), dairy products, alcohol, and coffee. If you still notice an especially strong smell, check with a doctor. Certain infections can cause a fishy smell.

"I was thinking about sex and being horny at a very young age, like seven or eight. I feel ashamed about it. Is it normal? I hope so."

It's totally normal to be curious about sex at a young age. Kids aged six to eight often have lots of questions about bodies and babies and even sex. Most people start actually experiencing being horny as they begin going through puberty, usually closer to their tweens and teens. You have nothing to be ashamed about; it is normal to be thinking about it and be curious about it! Kids who engage in sexual activity very young may do so out of trauma, but even so, that would still be nothing to be ashamed about. If you think you are acting out of trauma, seek help from a therapist.

"When I masturbate, I don't feel anything, nor do I have a sex drive."

There could be many reasons why someone might not feel something when they masturbate. One possible reason is that you may be asexual. Asexuality means not having typical sexual feelings and thoughts, and some asexual people do not have a desire to masturbate.

You may also be having trouble relaxing enough to enjoy masturbation properly. Some people find it is helpful to wear headphones or put on music to help them ignore the outside world. Some people find they need pictures or other forms of visuals or sounds to help them feel aroused first. If you haven't yet tried this, it could be helpful to try when you are relaxed, not rushed, and to see what helps you feel in the mood.

"Whenever I touch the head of my penis, it aches/burns. Is that normal?"

Your penis should not hurt to the touch. I recommend letting a doctor know so they can examine to see if there is any infection or inflammation.

"I am really young (11) and when I touch myself, I get a sensation like I have to pee but I don't actually have to pee. Is that normal?"

It is normal to interpret the pressure near our bladder as a feeling of needing to pee. If you are putting any pressure on the front wall of the vagina or the base of the penis, you might be sending pressure signals that your body misinterprets as a full bladder.

"Is masturbation as a 14-year-old girl safe and normal?"

Yes, masturbation is normal, safe, and healthy at any age, as long as you are hygienic about how you masturbate.

"I have these bumps on my penis and I have never had sex before. They go along the line of where I was circumcised and I don't know what to do. Any thoughts?"

This definitely sounds like a question for a doctor, so they can examine the penis and determine what is causing the bumps.

"Is it normal for me to be able to smell my vagina if I haven't showered for a few days?"

Yes; if you are not showering regularly, you will likely build up an odor around your genitals. This can also happen from dehydration or certain types of infections.

"What if you're born without a hymen?"

People are born with all different shaped and sized hymens, some so small they are barely there. People can also tear their hymen through any number of activities growing up. It's totally fine not to have a hymen.

"I smell super bad down there. I'm a virgin and no matter what I do it always smells and it's so embarrassing."

I'm sorry you are feeling embarrassed! Some people think their vagina smells bad when it just smells like a vagina! But if you really do have an odor issue, you should see your doctor. It could be something called bacterial vaginosis, even if you are a virgin. It could also indicate an infection. If you are using something other than mild soap and water to clean your vagina or fix the smell, you could be causing your pH balance to be off, which could then cause more of an odor.

If you have a penis, a smell from your genitals is most likely due to lack of proper hygiene. Be sure to clean daily beneath the foreskin if you have an uncircumcised penis.

It is also possible a smell could be due to an infection or skin condition. If you suspect this is the case, please speak to your doctor.

"Are inverted nipples normal?"

An inverted nipple is one that is flat or goes inward from the areola. They are normal and usually harmless. However, if you had outward nipples that then became inverted, that would be something to talk to a doctor about. Inverted nipples can make breastfeeding a bit more challenging, so if you are considering that, it would be a good idea to talk with a doctor about it.

"Is a lot of discharge normal? Is it normal if it smells bad?"

Discharge has all kinds of causes, including arousal, menstruation, or infection. Regular discharge is a sign that your reproductive system is working well. However, if yours is truly excessive or smells bad, that would be worth discussing with a doctor.

"Is it normal for tampons to get stuck inside of you?"

It does happen, and it's not typically too concerning. The cervix would not allow a tampon through, so it really can't get stuck far enough in to become lost inside of you. Be careful to find the right size tampon for your body, however, as having a tampon stuck inside of you increases your risk for developing toxic shock syndrome. If you can't remove it easily, it would be best to visit a doctor or a clinic so it doesn't stay in too long.

"Is there an age that's too young to read 'smut' or watch pornography?"

There is no set age for pornography, and it is normal to have interest in it. Preteens often read smut online on sites like Wattpad. It is also normal to have come across internet videos by accident as early as elementary school. It is important to make careful choices about what pornography you use. Think about whether or not what you are seeing is realistic—much of pornography shows unrealistic genitalia and has a sexist or unhealthy take on relationships. That doesn't make it bad by default, but it is important to be able to separate fantasy from reality.

"How do I know if I have a porn addiction? Is it normal to watch porn every time I masturbate?"

It is normal to use pornography to masturbate. Some reasons to be concerned, however, include not being able to control when you watch porn, feeling angry or irritable without it, if it is affecting your life negatively, if it is affecting your relationships, and/or you can't enjoy sexual activity without it. If this sounds like you, try cutting off some of your sources and reducing the amount of porn you consume.

"Is it normal for my penis to have a little bend in it when erect?"

Yes! It's totally normal for a penis to have a little bend in it. It's only concerning if it causes you any pain, in which case you should certainly talk with your doctor about it.

"I've never had an orgasm. When I massage my clitoris for a while it feels pleasurable, and I get very close to climaxing. But it becomes extremely sensitive at that point where I have to stop. It's really frustrating because it feels good but too good to the point where I cannot handle it, and clitoris stimulation is the only type of masturbation that feels pleasurable for me. Is that normal?"

It is normal to have difficulty orgasming, especially for those with a vagina. This question sounds to me like one of two things. Some people practice something called **edging** — they go right up to the point of climax and then stop, and then pick it up again later. Edging can be used to increase the eventual orgasm. You may be unintentionally edging, making it harder for you to achieve full orgasm, as the sensation becomes more and more to take. It is also common for people to have trouble letting go of control enough to allow the body to experience the orgasm. If you find you are trying to maintain control, you could try masturbating when no one is home and you don't feel as much need to maintain control in order to stay quiet.

Chapter 2

Sex
*(Only Your Teachers
Call It "Intercourse")*

*L*et me introduce the main character of this book: s-e-x
(*gasp*). Sex is most often defined as penetration by a
penis into a vagina. This definition, however, excludes much
of the LGBTQIA+ community (what counts as lesbian sex, for
example? Are gay people just **virgins** forever?). It also leaves
out the necessary element of **consent**. Consent is the active
permission for something to happen; when it comes to sexual
activity, consent should never be assumed.

Defining sex

So like the *girlboss* I am (yes, I'm being purposefully cringy),
I decided to make my own definition of sex.

> **Sexual activity:** any nonplatonic physical touch that is con-
> sensual and meant to create pleasure. This means kissing,
> fondling, caressing, stroking, rubbing, and oral stimulation
> (using your mouth). While not all sexual activity is consid-
> ered sex, there is a lot of overlap.

One of the most common questions we received in our question box was, "At what point of sexual activity am I no longer a virgin?"

The reason I don't *love* this question is because I am not a fan of the concept of **virginity**. Virginity is the idea that one has never had sex. Virginity is often associated with moral purity, a way of shaming women into not having sex even when they are physically, emotionally, and mentally ready. It is also used to create peer pressure to have sex when *not* ready.

While I am not a fan of the focus on virginity, I do understand the desire to know if you have had sex or not. In order to answer this incredibly common question, I am proposing a new definition of sex:

> **Sex/sexual intercourse**: any consensual physical touch involving two or more people that has the goal of at least one person having an orgasm through their genitals, whether or not an orgasm is actually achieved.

Orgasm

During sex, there is a buildup of pressure inside your body, an intensity of feeling that comes from your nerves and from your emotions. An orgasm is when all the intensely pleasurable feelings suddenly relax. It is often called "cumming." Orgasms release endorphins in your body, which is why they feel so good. An orgasm is definitely not the only way to enjoy sex, but it is typically the most intense.

Orgasms are usually achieved through stimulation of the genitals (clitoris, vagina, penis, testicles, and anus), although people often find they have other sensitive areas on their body as well, such as nipples, inner thighs, and ears. Some people can experience orgasm solely from stimulation of their nipples or even from intense sexual thoughts. It is healthy and natural to explore various parts of your body to see what feels good to you.

Orgasms can happen during masturbation or sex. Masturbation is when someone stimulates their genitals themself. This can be done by hand or with hygienic and safe sex toys, such as vibrators.

An orgasm with a penis is typically accompanied by ejaculation of about one to two tablespoons of semen (slang: *cum*). This semen is the fluid that carries the sperm. After orgasming, the penis goes from erect to relaxed. The penis can also return to being relaxed without orgasming.

Orgasms from the vagina are not as straightforward. People with vaginas can experience orgasms in a wide variety of ways, which makes the experience hard to define. It can also take a variety of types of stimulation for people to orgasm from a vagina, and it can take longer than with a penis. It takes on average from about 10–20 minutes for a person to orgasm from their vagina, making an orgasm unlikely if you are squeezing in a "quickie" without much foreplay. This is why it is more common for people with vaginas to fake an orgasm.

♥ I have been with my partner for about six months, and I still fake my orgasms way more than I actually cum. I thought by now we'd be better at sex, but I'm not really sure how to have better orgasms. Part of it is my fault I guess—I fake a lot of my orgasms just so that she feels good about making me cum, but that's not really teaching her what *actually* works for me. Sometimes I get so bored or distracted during sex I

> just fake my orgasm to be done. I don't know if she is doing
> the same thing...we're both pretty inexperienced, and I don't
> really know how to talk to her about it.

Some physical signs of orgasm include a rush of very intense and pleasurable feelings, contractions in the genitals, and increased breathing and heart rates. Some people describe it as an aching need that increases and then suddenly decreases. The vagina typically becomes more lubricated ("wet") close to orgasm, and some people ejaculate fluid from their vagina after orgasming ("squirting").

If you have trouble orgasming, there are things that could be affecting your ability to do so. These could be physical, such as hormones, health, medications, alcohol, or drugs. They could also be emotional or mental. Some people struggle with shame, insecurity, fear, past experiences, or stress.

Sex is not *only* about the orgasm. Not everyone orgasms every time they have sex. Try to keep in mind it doesn't mean you aren't "into" your partner, or that you are "bad" at sex. If you'd like to improve your orgasms, it is healthy and natural to experiment to see what feels best for your specific body. Ideally, sexual intimacy is not a race but rather more of a joyride; the pleasure you experience along the way is just as important as reaching your destination.

A bit more on virginity

As I mentioned, the idea of virginity is often used to shame people about sex, or to pressure them into it. I believe sex should be something you engage in only when physically, mentally, emotionally, and practically ready to handle all the implications of your decision...every time you have sex. And then I believe it is something that should be enjoyed guilt and shame free, once you are ready.

The concept of virginity often focuses on purity and places those who have had premarital sex into derogatory categories like "slut" or "whore." Parents often pressure their daughters to maintain their virginity. Peers, on the other hand, often pressure people to *lose* their virginity in order to avoid being labeled a "prude," or simply not cool enough to "get some."

♥ I grew up with deeply religious parents. One of the most important values they ingrained into me was purity and abstaining from sex until I got married. I went to a religious high school and, to my shock, everyone there was having sex—oral sex, anal sex, handjobs, pretty much anything except for penis-in-vagina sex. In my junior year, we even had a chlamydia outbreak, despite everyone at the school insisting they were waiting until marriage. Our sex ed only ever covered penis-in-vagina sex, so nobody thought there could be any consequences from other types of sexual activity, and because of this, nobody used any sort of protection.

The concept of virginity not only contributes to gender inequality but also is typically heteronormative (centered on heterosexuality). Losing one's virginity usually refers solely to penis-in-vagina sex, which as we've talked about is a very problematic definition of sex. This adds to the erasure of other sexualities and experiences.

Contrary to popular myth, there is no physical manifestation of virginity. The hymen is often pictured as this protective layer of skin covering the entire vaginal opening, and it is almost seen as a reward for the person "worthy" enough to break it. In actuality, the hymen usually doesn't cover the entire vaginal opening, and is often broken through other childhood activities, such as sports or tampon use. This myth can be extremely damaging in places where a woman might be beaten (or worse) for not being a virgin on her wedding night. If the breaking of her hymen doesn't cause spotting, it might be assumed that she had premarital sex, which in some areas is legally punishable.

♥ I'm a cisgender girl and I've been a dancer since I was eight years old, which means I've done a lot of splits, stretches, and jumps. Recently, I felt comfortable enough to have penis-in-vagina sex for the first time with my long-term girlfriend (she's AMAB). We expected there to be a bit of blood as my hymen broke, and we were completely shocked when there wasn't. Now she thinks I lied about being a virgin and is a bit hurt because she thinks I was untruthful. I don't know how to convince her that I probably broke my hymen dancing, because she keeps insisting that sex is the only thing that can break your hymen.

Despite not wanting to promote the concept of virginity, I am a teacher at heart and can't leave questions unanswered. So to answer your most asked questions about virginity:

- Masturbation does not typically count as "losing your virginity."
- Popping your cherry is an expression that means losing your vaginal virginity.
- If your hymen tears in other ways before you have sex, that does not mean you lost your virginity.
- If you are abused or have sex without consent, you are still a virgin (as sex is an act that *must* be consensual, or it is not sex).

Am I ready?

Choosing to have sex for the first time is a big decision, one that most people do not take lightly. There is a lot to consider, which is why the decision is so deeply personal. While only you can make the choice, it can be really helpful to have trusted adults, family, and friends to talk to about it. Being able to maturely and comfortably discuss sex is an important component of being ready to have sex.

♥ I'm a cis male senior in high school, and I just turned eighteen a few weeks ago. I've definitely had a sex drive and experienced sexual attraction for a couple of years now, but I've never really felt "ready" in the same way everyone else seems to have. I don't want to go to college as a virgin, and everyone else my age has been bragging about their "body count" for years. I figured that I was never going to feel any more ready than this. When I tried to bring it up to my boyfriend, though, I got really flustered and couldn't even bring myself to say the word "sex." I just can't talk about it—protection, STIs, any of it. I probably do need to wait until I can talk about sex comfortably in order to actually have sex. I hate how insecure it makes me to still be a virgin.

The pros of having sex are fairly straightforward; *if you are ready for it*, sex is a pleasurable activity that often helps couples feel more connected. It can have numerous health benefits, and it releases hormones that improve mood and decrease stress.

Sex also has a lot of risks. The most obvious ones include physical risks, such as **STIs**, **STDs** (sexually transmitted diseases), and unwanted pregnancies. But just as important are the emotional risks. It can create stress, anxiety, and feelings of sadness, loss, anger, or regret to have sex before you are ready. The same is true about having sex with someone you don't trust or respect, or who doesn't trust or respect you. Other things that might factor into your decision include your own morals and values, your family values, and your goals in life. For many people, it is really important to them that they be in a healthy and committed relationship before having sex.

One of the questions I ask teens to help them decide is, "Why do you want to have sex?" Very few people in high school have an emotionally mature response, one that shows actual readiness. A lot of people want to have sex because they assume "everyone else is doing it." The truth is the average age to begin having sex is 17, and less than half of high schoolers have sex. Even the teens who do have sex in high school often have sex infrequently. And many teens report wishing they had waited to have sex until later.

Some other reasons I have heard include, "I'm the only virgin left," "I want to get it over with," "My partner will leave me if we don't have sex," "It will make me more popular," or "It will make me feel older." These reasons all concern me because of the emotional ramifications of having sex before you truly want to. You will have the healthiest sex life if you wait until you are truly ready for all the emotional and physical consequences.

What is the first time like?

The most common question we get about the first time is, "Does it hurt?" This is usually a question people ask about vaginal penetration specifically. Everyone's experience is different. For some people there is some pain; for others there isn't. There may be some bleeding or spotting, though not for everyone. The first time should still be pleasurable beyond the initial pain, though it might be more painful if you are very nervous, as the anxiety will cause your vagina not to lubricate or expand as well. Try to take time with your first sexual experience, to allow yourself to relax and feel comfortable with each step that is happening.

One of the sweetest questions in our question box was this one: "How can I help my partner *not* have their first time be painful?" That question warmed my heart. Everyone should have a partner who is thinking about their experience with so much care. There is a lot that you can do to help someone have their best possible first experience. It should never be rushed, and as you move from one step to the next, check in frequently to make sure your partner is still enjoying themself and still ready for more. If you are preparing for vaginal penetration, you can use lubrication to help make sure the vagina is ready, and you can help expand the vagina with fingers and/or oral sex before penis or dildo penetration.

A lot of people want to know if the first time is "awkward." It certainly can be, and that's nothing to be ashamed of! It's something new, and with all new things, there may be some clumsiness or misunderstandings. Try to get over the awkwardness by laughing it off together, and use it as a way to bring you and your partner together. Then pick back up by starting with foreplay you are more comfortable with.

♥ I remember the first time I had sex, I was really nervous about lasting long enough. They show it all the time in movies and stuff, the guy ejaculating before even doing much at all. I masturbated a lot beforehand, thinking that might build up my stamina. I didn't even really enjoy it as much because it felt like I was in training or something. Then when it was time to actually do it, I was so awkward. I was trying to be all like, sexy, but I didn't really know what I was doing. My girlfriend started laughing and I almost died, but she actually helped me a lot. She called me out about being nervous and said she was nervous too, and that she wasn't going to judge me or our relationship based on our first time having sex. She said something sweet like, "Just kiss me and we'll figure out the rest." It wasn't great sex, but it felt really good for me, and it definitely got better for her over time.

One person wrote into the question box that they are "scared" for their first time. My initial reaction was that if you are feeling scared, you are probably not ready, and that it's okay to not be ready. But scared can mean a lot of different things. If you are slightly anxious, that's perfectly normal, and my only advice would be to communicate that to your partner. But if you are feeling actual fear, I would view that as a red flag. Take time to understand that fear—is it about your partner, your body image, past trauma, cultural pressures, or something else?

A lot of people feel even more anxious about their first time after watching pornography, believing that's what sex should look like. Most of what happens in porn is extremely unrealistic. Porn is useful to some people for getting in the mood for sex or masturbation, but it is not what you should expect from sex in general.

Communication

One of the most important parts of a healthy sex life is having strong communication between partners. Take time to check in with each other about commitment levels and expectations about sexual intimacy. Be sure to establish consent each time you have sex. Just because you have sex once doesn't mean you want to the next time, and it's okay to be in the mood sometimes and not others.

It is also important to remember that you have other important relationships in your life other than your sexual partner(s). Be sure to have conversations with friends and family to make sure you maintain your support system. It is up to you if you want to share your sex life with anyone, but it can be helpful to have people to talk to about it other than your partner.

Types of sex

Important: The descriptions below are sexually explicit. If they are difficult for you to read, or make you feel uncomfortable, I recommend you skip the rest of this chapter and come back to it later.

Not everyone participates in all forms of sex. You should never let anyone pressure you into doing something that makes you uncomfortable. It is perfectly okay to never want some or all of the forms of physical touch detailed below.

Rather than get into details of each sexuality or gender combination, I will discuss sex in terms of body parts. I will use mostly the correct anatomical terms, while being fully aware that you probably use slang for most of the words I'm about to write.

Sex typically involves people consensually "turning each other on," meaning making each other aroused, through a combination of touch and voice. This is known as **foreplay**. When a vagina is aroused, it self-lubricates, which is important because it makes sex feel pleasurable rather than forced or painful. People sometimes add additional store-bought lubricants to increase wetness. Sex toys can be used to increase pleasure during sex. Only use objects that are designed to be safe for sex, and keep any toys you use clean after every use.

If using lube, it is important to get the right kind. Certain lubes can't be used along with sex toys and/or condoms. Water-based lubricants are great—they usually don't stain, and they wash off easily. Silicone-based lubricants are better for sensitive skin and are more long lasting, but they can remove the protective surface of certain sex toys, making it easier for bacteria to grow on them. Oil-based lubes are enjoyed for being long lasting and slick, but they shouldn't be used with condoms and they can stain sheets and clothing. They also carry a higher risk of causing a yeast infection. Spermicidal lubricants can be inserted into the vagina before sex to help prevent pregnancy. These are about 70 percent effective and can be combined with other birth control methods. They work by slowing down sperm.

When a penis gets aroused, it becomes erect. This makes it longer, makes it stiff, and pulls it away from the body. Lubricants can be applied to the penis or on top of a condom if desired, as long as it is the right type of lube. Lube can also be used on the vagina. Penis-in-vagina sex involves inserting the penis into the vagina.

Some people are scared they will "put it in the wrong hole." The vagina naturally lubricates and expands when aroused, making it easy to distinguish from the urethra (where pee comes out of) and the anus. The urethra and anus are both much smaller holes than the vaginal opening, and do not self-lubricate. It would be very difficult to accidentally use the wrong hole.

As consent is extremely important, it should be made clear that each person is ready for sex, and that everything is feeling good and pleasurable to all partners. It is totally normal to check in with your partner to make sure they are enjoying themself—in fact, questions like "Do you like this?" are often considered a turn-on.

Another way to have penetrative sex is with a sex toy like a dildo. If used properly, this can simulate the feeling of penetration for those who desire that. There are many different types of dildos. Some are vibrator/dildo combinations, some can be used with a strap-on harness (this allows someone with a vagina to simulate having a penis), some are curved to hit the G-spot, some are straight for easier thrusting, and some are thicker or thinner than others. There are even some that ejaculate lubricant.

Oral sex involves using one's mouth and/or tongue to pleasure a partner. Slang for oral sex includes "going down" on someone, "blowjobs," "head," "munching," or "eating [someone] out." Oral sex is a form of sex, with the goal of creating an orgasm. People use their mouth on breasts (nipples), the clitoris, the vulva, the vagina, the penis, and the anus (known as rimming). Oral sex can easily transmit STIs, so it is just as important to be safe and use protection during oral sex as it is during penis-in-vagina penetrative sex. An example of protection for use during oral sex is a dental dam, which is a thin and flexible piece of latex that provides an effective barrier.

Another way of making someone cum, or orgasm, is by using your hands. Some people participate in mutual masturbation, where they take turns making the other person have an orgasm while only using their hands. People often do this because they don't count it as sex, but according to my definition, this would still be a form of sex. Mutual masturbation actually has a second definition. It can also mean masturbating in front of your partner while they do the same.

Some people rub their vaginas together in order to orgasm, a technique known as **scissoring**. It's called scissoring because of the way you need to spread and intertwine your legs to accomplish this. This is commonly associated with the lesbian community, along with what is lovingly referred to as the "knee thing." This is when one partner unintentionally (or intentionally) lifts their knee up toward their partner's vagina, rubbing it gently in order to stimulate their clitoris.

Another form of sex is **anal** penetrative sex (penis or dildo in anus). It is extremely important to learn how to do this properly, as the anus does not expand and lubricate on its own. People often need to prepare ahead of time by emptying their bowels out. Doing this naturally is completely fine; it is not necessary to douche. If you do use a douche product, be sure to only use it once or twice a week. Next, the anus needs to be slowly massaged and warmed up to be able to properly fit the penis or dildo. Use a dental dam to protect your mouth if practicing rimming, which is using your mouth to stimulate the anus. Lubrication is essential for safe anal sex, because the anus does not produce any natural lubrication. Be sure to use a condom to protect yourself from STIs or infection from bacteria. Never have vaginal sex after anal sex without fully washing yourself.

Sex toys

Sex toys are objects people use to increase pleasure during sex. Some people use them and some don't, and both are totally normal. Be sure to use ones that are designed to be safe for use during sex, and to keep it clean and hygienic.

Here are some of the most common ones:

Vibrators: this is an object that vibrates. People use that vibration to stimulate their body. Vibrators are most commonly used on the clitoris, but can also be used around the vulva, nipples, penis, scrotum, and anus. Some people find the vibration pleasurable in other parts of their body as well. Some vibrators can also penetrate, while others do not. Some are waterproof but many are not, so do not assume you can use your vibrator in the shower or in water without checking.

Dildos: these are often shaped like a penis and are most commonly used to penetrate into a vagina or anus.

Strap-ons: also called harnesses, these are materials that hold a sex toy on your body, such as a dildo or a packer.

Penis rings: these are rings that go on the base of the penis to reduce blood flow. This can help to increase sensation, which then makes the erection harder and more long lasting. It is really important to remove these after 10–30 minutes, or if you feel any pain or discomfort.

Packers: these are designed to help people with a vagina create the feeling of having a penis. Some of them can help you stand to pee, and some can be used for sex.

Anal toys: this is a collection of objects created specifically for anal stimulation. You need to use lubrication on these, and it is very important that the base is wide enough to stop one from accidentally going all the way into the anus. If that happens, you would need to go to a doctor to have it removed.

Transgender sex

Transgender sex mostly looks just like sex as detailed above. However, there are some differences. One of the biggest is about body **dysphoria**. A trans man born with breasts, for example, may feel dysphoric if his breasts are fondled during sex. A different trans man may not mind at all, and a third may sometimes find it pleasurable and sometimes upsetting. It is important to have strong communication with a trans partner about what touches feel good, just like with all partners.

♥ I've been out as a trans woman for years now, and though I'm comfortable with most parts of my body (still occasionally dysphoric, but estrogen has really helped), my penis still gives me a lot of dysphoria. I haven't had a partner for a while, and I'm not really one to hook up with people, but I recently had sex for the first time in almost a year with someone I really trust and love. He's a trans man, which was nice because we both understood what each other needed. Generally, I'm not comfortable with my penis having any sort of pleasure, and he doesn't prefer to have his breasts touched, so I typically finger him or have oral sex. He usually uses a strap-on to have anal sex with me.

Some transgender people prefer to keep certain articles of clothing on during sex. This is totally fine, except that a binder should never be worn during physical activity (see Chapter 5 for more on binders). Some people prefer the lights to be off or to be under blankets to avoid seeing the parts of their body that give them feelings of dysphoria. Notice what gives you or your partner feelings of gender euphoria and focus on that. Refer to your and your partner's anatomy with the terms that feel most gender aligned—for instance, many AFAB trans men refer to "breasts" as "chests" with extra chest tissue.

Tops, bottoms, and switches (or verses)

These are terms that are used within the queer community to refer to sexual preferences. **Tops** are usually the ones penetrating during sex—penis, fingers, tongue, and/or sex toys. **Bottoms** are the ones receiving, though it is important to recognize that by receiving, one is usually giving their partner pleasure too.

Top is also sometimes used to refer to the person who enjoys being the more dominant person during sex, while bottoms often prefer to follow their lead. Tops tend to be more in control of what is happening during sex, and more active during sex, often preferring to do the penetration or giving oral sex and not preferring to receive these acts.

A **verse** is a term typically only used in the gay community to discuss giving and receiving. A **switch** is someone who can be dominant or submissive.

These descriptors are becoming increasingly common on dating sites and social media as a way to help clue in the queer community to find good sexual matches. As well as being helpful, however, there is also a fair amount of shaming that goes on with these terms. "Bottom shaming," for example, is shaming someone for never wanting to give oral sex or penetration, with the implication this makes them "less queer." Such shaming is harmful, as it perpetuates harmful stereotypes.

Anonymous sex ed question box

"What does the hymen look like?"

Hymens don't all look the same way. Some stretch across

the vaginal opening like a thin disk, some look like a crescent or half-moon, some make a ring around the vagina. There is no "one" look that is right.

"Is anyone else insecure about their body while having sex?"

Lots of people are. This is a really common insecurity, so much so that many people refuse to let their partner see their body. They may keep the lights off, stay under blankets, or keep some clothes on to avoid the feeling of insecurity.

The most important thing to do is talk to your partner about how you feel. A supportive partner will help reassure you that you are sexy to them. Ask your partner to make comments about your body that help you to accept and love yourself. They may give you other compliments too, like, "I love how it feels when you lay pressed next to me" or "You smell amazing."

If your insecurity is extreme, a therapist could be helpful. Overcoming body insecurity is a gradual process. You can't just convince yourself not to care; you have to speak kindly to yourself day after day until you begin to believe what you say.

"I'm really insecure, and when the time is right I feel like I might just turn it down because I'm scared of what they will think of my body."

You are not alone in being insecure about your partner seeing your body. I often still feel like that, and I've been married over 20 years! There are so many societal messages about our bodies not being good enough. Almost everyone has parts of their body they dislike, which is such a shame. In my experience, most people don't feel that way about their partner's bodies. Sex is often so much more about the connection you create than the perfection of the body itself.

It could help to talk to your partner about your insecurities. Give them a chance to be there for you — they might make you feel so much better about yourself. You can also take things at your own pace — if you need to leave some clothing on at first, that's okay. I hope one day you feel comfortable with your body whatever it looks like, but it's completely natural for that to take time.

If you can't move past the fear of what your partner will think about your body, it's possible you just aren't feeling safe enough yet in the relationship to be having sex. Trust yourself and be kind to yourself.

"Do I have to shave my pubes for sex?"

Absolutely not — not if you don't want to. There is no reason you have to shave, wax, or trim your pubic hair for sex. Some people choose to for looks, or because they or their partner prefer the feeling of it being shorter. But many people do not care if their partner has pubic hair that is long or short, and the decision ultimately should be your own. Pubic hair serves a purpose — it actually protects the vagina from bacteria and debris. It can also help by reducing the friction of skin-to-skin contact. If you do want to shave, wax, or trim, that is also totally fine!

"I scissored my girlfriend and I'm wondering if that counts as losing my V card?"

If you participated in scissoring, that would count as sex by my definition. It is stimulation of the genitals with the goal of creating pleasure and/or orgasm.

"Is it possible for someone to tell if you've had sex before?"

It is not possible to tell upon physical examination that you have had sex before unless you contract an STI or become pregnant.

"Why can I only orgasm when I masturbate and not during sex?"

There are many possible reasons that this may be happening. The first one that occurs to me is that you might be anxious or self-conscious during sex. That is quite common, especially if you are young or new to sex. It is more difficult to orgasm if you are unable to relax your mind and/or release control.

Another possibility is that your partner may not be as good as you are at "turning you on." If this is the case, communication can help a lot. Let them know what feels the best to you, and don't be afraid to keep letting them know until they learn what makes you orgasm. It is often a turn-on for people to be told what makes you feel pleasure. It doesn't always have to be verbal; you can also (consensually!) direct your partner's hands and/or mouth and/or genitals where you want them to go.

One other answer is that you may be asexual and not feel full sexual attraction to others in a typical way. This is discussed more in the chapter on sexuality.

"Is there something wrong if you are a girl and you only dry orgasm?"

Not at all! Not all people with vaginas "squirt" or ejaculate during orgasm. Less than half report doing so on the reports I have read.

"Can a woman (or someone with a vagina) have an orgasm without touching the clit or is that the only way?"

Yes. Women can orgasm from different points on their body. The clitoris is the most common one, but people have reported orgasming from nipple stimulation, anal sex, or even from extremely intense sexual thoughts.

"What does cum look like? For girls and boys?"

For people with a vagina, ejaculation is less frequent. It looks like a whitish fluid that is slightly thicker than water. For people with a penis, semen is ejaculated during most orgasms. It is a whitish-gray fluid that is thicker than female ejaculate, with a jelly-like consistency.

"Do people actually swallow cum?"

Yes, some people do choose to. It is considered generally safe, though you should always be aware of STIs. And you should never feel pressured to if you don't want to.

"Is it normal to not 'finish' during sex? I've never had an orgasm."

It's totally normal to not orgasm during sex. There are lots of reasons that might happen, and if you are someone with a vagina, it is not always straightforward to know how to have an orgasm. If you'd like to orgasm, it could help to explore what feels the best to you through masturbation, if that is something you enjoy. It is important to then communicate that to your partner.

Many people don't orgasm because they don't allow for enough time to climax properly. Some are afraid of "asking for too much" during sex. You should know that most people find it a turn-on to have you ask for things that feel extra good to you. Sometimes people are stressed or anxious and have trouble relaxing their mind and body enough to orgasm.

"What do you do after you finish? How will my partner know? Then what do you do after that?"

Your body usually will give signs that it has orgasmed, which is one way that your partner will likely know. This might look like body spasms or contractions, and your breathing will often become more rapid or strained and then relax. The intensity of movement will generally suddenly slow down quite a bit. After that, it depends on your relationship with your partner. Some people cuddle, some people go their separate ways, some people fall asleep.

"What if she wants to use a toy but it hasn't been cleaned since the last partner and she is begging?"

Sex toys can easily transmit STIs if they aren't cleaned after each use. Out of respect and care for your partner, you should not use the toy until it has been cleaned, no matter how in the mood or horny you or she is feeling. Other than STIs, you also want to protect your partner from random bacteria or debris.

"Is it okay to have e-sex/internet sex?"

Many people do use phones or the internet to have sex, especially if they have a partner who doesn't live nearby. While this type of sex has no immediate physical risk, it does have privacy risks, as well as emotional ones.

One risk is an adult disguising themself as a teen in order to talk with younger kids. They may try to get kids involved in pornography, prostitution, sex, or other illegal activities. You should never give out any identifying information online, and you should never agree to meet someone you have met online without proper supervision. Another risk is someone recording you or taking screenshots.

"Is it okay to send nudes?"

This is a personal decision, and all I can do is let you know the risks so you can make the best decision for you. The main risk is your "digital footprint," which is the idea that everything you do digitally can be found by others later. Many people have put trust in the wrong person only to have their private photos end up in the public eye or to be blackmailed with them later. Once you put an image out there in cyberspace, you immediately lose all control over that image. People like to think it won't happen to them, but I think you should accept that everyone might possibly see the image, and then decide if you are okay with that as a possible outcome. Even using apps like Snapchat, which alerts you if someone takes a screenshot, is not fully safe; someone could easily use another device to take a photo of your photo rather than screenshot it.

Sexting can also have legal risks. In many areas, sharing photos of a naked or partially naked minor's body, even your own, even amongst teens in a relationship, is considered child sex abuse and could be a felony. Some states have sexting-specific laws. It can be a crime to have these photos, even if you didn't request them.

"Are you supposed to bleed during sex and after?"

It is common to notice some bleeding (often just spotting) from your vagina the first time you have sex. This is typically due to some tearing of the hymen. It is also totally normal not to bleed the first time, as your hymen may have been already torn through activities in your childhood.

If it is not your first time and you still notice bleeding during or after sex, it is a good idea to let a medical professional know. It could be nothing at all worrisome, but you won't know for sure without a medical examination. The doctor may want to check if your cervix is healthy. It is also possible for bleeding to occur because of vaginal dryness, being near your period, or STIs.

"How often is too much sex? Is it normal to want it every day?"

People have all different sex drives, and there is no "normal" when it comes to how often you enjoy having sex. However, there are some reasons to be concerned: If you feel angry or irritable without it, if it is affecting your life negatively (for example, your grades), and/or if it is affecting your relationships. If it's all you can think about and your life is suffering because of that, that's a problem. Otherwise, there is no such thing as "too much" sex.

"Is it okay to cry and have a panic attack during sex? It happened to me one time so far and I'm not sure if it's normal."

You are not alone in experiencing strong emotions during sex, including strong feelings of anxiety. Some reasons may include past trauma or negative experiences, stress, insecurities, or performance anxiety. Be open with your partner about how you are feeling, and perhaps explore other, less intense, types of sexual activity to increase your comfort with being physical.

"Is it normal to feel the man's penis while it's in you? Sometimes I feel a weird stretching during it; is that normal?"

Yes, it is normal to be able to feel that you have a penis in your vagina. If the sensations are pleasurable, it is likely all normal. If you feel sensations that are painful, that is important to discuss with your partner and perhaps a doctor.

"My partner likes to be choked. How can I do this safely?"

Choking during sex is extremely dangerous and carries many risks. There is no completely safe way to practice this. This is not the same as spanking, or light bondage, which are other kinks. It is really dangerous.

Many people are under the impression this can be done safely. It can be done *more* safely or *less* safely, but it is never actually safe. And there is no way to make it safer when choking oneself.

As many people do not fully understand that choking is always dangerous, they may not be giving proper consent to choking. It is important if you are going to engage in this that all involved understand the real risks. Minor risks include broken blood vessels in the face, a hoarse voice, or trouble swallowing. Severe risks include brain damage and death.

"What if I'm too scared to try something, but I want to try it to see if I like it? What if it's weird?"

Everything you do during sex should be something that feels good and that you want. So if you are feeling slight fear but *mostly* excitement, that might be worth exploring. If you feel some excitement but *mostly* fear, perhaps it is something you are not into or ready for. You could try to figure out what your fears are and research if they are realistic. Generally, an acceptable feeling of being a little scared during sex comes from the fear of something being so intensely pleasurable it overwhelms you. To me, an unacceptable fear would be of doing something with serious risk of harm.

And chances are, if it's something you enjoy, it's not that weird. People enjoy all kinds of things when it comes to sex. Just be sure it is something safe for you and your partner, and that it is consensual.

"What is phone sex?"

Phone sex is an example of people using only their voice to help their partner feel turned on. People sometimes do this over texting too—telling their partner what they would like to be doing to their body. People may also choose to do this on a video call, but you need to be really careful with that one. Just like nude images can never truly be recovered once they are out there, the same is true of a recording or screenshot someone might take during phone sex. Remember that even apps like Snapchat are not fully safe because someone can use another device to take a photo of your photo.

"Are nipple clamps dangerous?"

If used improperly they can be, but they are usually not. It is important to buy a high-quality nipple clamp, ideally one that allows for adjustment. It is also important to have a lot of communication to make sure your partner is still consenting and okay with anything you do to them.

Risks would include irritation to the breast tissue, pain that is more severe than desired, and lack of enough blood flow to the nipples. This usually would take time to happen, so it shouldn't be an issue with good communication and attention.

"How do I say no to sending nude pictures?"

Sending nude photos is something you should definitely consider carefully. Once you send a photo, it is always possible that people other than the person you intended the photo for will see it—I encourage everyone to take their digital footprint seriously. Sometimes people don't want to send a nude photo for other reasons—it just makes them uncomfortable. Whatever the reason, I am glad you are listening to your own feelings and needs. Hopefully your partner will be too. All you need to do is let them know how it makes you feel. That might be, "I love that you find me hot, but I don't feel comfortable putting nude photos of me out there." Or perhaps, "It makes me feel uncomfortable taking and sending nude pics, but I love when we..."

Your partner might pressure you, even subtly. They might say, "You can trust me. I would never share the picture," or something of the sort. You should never allow yourself to be pressured into things you are uncomfortable with. The truth is, nude pictures often do make it out into the larger world.

If you are a minor, under the legal age of adulthood, it is actually illegal in many parts of the world to take and send nude photos. It is considered child pornography, and it can even get you registered as a sex offender and/or charged with a felony.

"How and where do you put lube on a female?"

There are many different ways lube can be used to enhance sex. The most straightforward is applying lube to the labia to ease friction during penetration. If using your fingers for penetration, apply it to your fingers. Many people apply lube to sex toys before using them. Some condoms come with lubrication on them as well. Lube should always be used during anal sex.

Chapter 3

Yes, Yes, Yes
(Understanding Consent)

his is one of the most important chapters in this book, but also could be a very triggering one. Too many people, of *all* genders, have had experiences with **sexual harassment**, **assault**, **abuse**, and **rape**. If you have ever been sexually touched without your consent, I am so deeply sorry. It wasn't fair or right, and it absolutely wasn't your fault.

There are many resources available to help you, including the National Sexual Assault Hotline (1-800-656-4673) from RAINN (online.rainn.org). It can be very difficult to talk about these experiences, but I hope you can find the support you need. If this subject is triggering for you, it is okay to skip over it and jump to the next chapter. Just know that sexual touch without consent is never okay.

What is consent?

Consent means freely agreeing to something. In the case of sex, consent means freely agreeing to any and all sexual contact. It is important to obtain consent for each and every sexual act, every time. Not gaining consent could be deemed sexual assault or rape.

♥ I was hanging out with my partner in my apartment. We got pretty drunk, and her and I both agreed enthusiastically to have sex. The night after, though, both of us felt really gross about it — we knew we weren't going to get pregnant or anything because we're both AFAB — but we'd been planning on waiting a little bit longer before having sex. Neither of us assaulted each other, but neither of us consented either, because we weren't in a mental state where we could consent. I felt in a really weird place for a while, because neither of us were taking advantage of the other, and yet both of us felt violated. I've felt pretty averse to and scared of any sort of touch since then, so me and my partner are both going to a sex and relationships therapist to talk about it and work through it.

Planned Parenthood has an acronym to help explain consent: FRIES.

Freely given: It's not okay to pressure, trick, or threaten someone into saying yes. And you can't give consent if you're drunk, high, or passed out.

Reversible: It's okay to say yes and then change your mind— at any time! Even if you've done it before, and even if you're both naked in bed.

Informed: You can only consent to something if you have all the facts. For example, if someone says they'll use a condom and then they don't, there isn't full consent.

Enthusiastic: When it comes to sex, you should do stuff you WANT to do, not things people expect you to do. If someone doesn't seem enthusiastic (meaning happy, excited, or energized), stop and check in.

Specific: Saying yes to one thing (like going to the bedroom to make out) doesn't mean you're saying yes to other things (like having sex).

If someone is drunk, high, asleep, passed out, below the legal age, much younger than you, or disabled in a way that affects their ability to understand you, they are not able to give consent.

How do I ask for and give consent?

A lot of people wonder how to ask for consent. They envision stopping every few minutes and asking, "Do I have your consent to continue?" That could definitely dampen the mood. Consent can be more subtle than that, but it is still important that it is *clear* and *enthusiastic*. Ask questions like "Do you like this?" and "Does this feel good?"

If you want to let someone know that you consent to what they are doing, you can actively do so, which can take the burden off of them to keep checking in. There are many ways to let someone know you want them to continue what they are doing, such as exclamations of delight ("Yes, please, that feels so good...").

♥ When I am dating someone, I never just grab them and kiss them. I pull them in close and say something like, "I'm going to kiss you now." I then wait to see if they pull away or smile and turn their lips to me for a kiss. That's my sign that they are okay with what is happening. If they seem hesitant, I pull back and tell them we don't have to go there yet. As we start doing more sexually, I'll usually check in every time I do something new. I'll ask, "Do you like this?" or "You want this?" I love that checking in with them means I get to hear them say yes to me, which is such a turn-on.

How do I say no?

If someone asks for consent, and you are not interested, it is natural to worry about disappointing them or hurting their feelings, especially if you like them. But it is important that you protect yourself as well, and that you look out for your own emotional health. You can say things like "I'm not ready for that" or "I'm not in the mood today."

If someone initiates sexual activity without asking for consent, simply tell them no or stop. Don't allow them to pressure you into something you don't want to do. And if you say no or stop and they keep going, that is sexual assault. Even if you eventually give in and say yes, it is *still* assault because the yes was not "freely given." Do whatever you need to do to remove yourself safely from the situation, and then reach out for support. You might let a supervisory adult know or contact a sexual assault center, such as RAINN.

What are the laws about consent?

Laws about consent are different everywhere. It is important that you become familiar with the laws in your area. As mentioned, there are situations where a person is unable to give consent, due to age or cognitive ability.

One thing that is true almost everywhere is that it is never too late to take consent back. If someone becomes uncomfortable at any point, they can ask you to stop. Legally, anything beyond that point becomes assault.

The difference between sexual harassment, assault, and rape depends on location. Harassment usually does not involve physical contact. Assault is any sexual activity that is not consensual. Rape usually means forced vaginal, anal, or oral penetration by a body part or object. All rape is a type of assault, but not all assaults are rape.

Some examples of sexual assault include:

- someone touching your genitals or breasts without your consent
- someone showing you their genitals and/or making you touch them without consent
- someone rubbing their genitals against you (grinding) without consent
- someone forcing you to kiss them
- someone restraining you in order to touch you sexually.

Content warning: Assault/attempted rape

♥ When I was 16, I started fooling around with my boyfriend more than I ever had before with anyone. I didn't really know much about sex, and he had more experience than me. So I kind of just let him lead the way. Well one day we were really horny and making out in his basement, and he put my hand on his penis. He said I was so hot and had him "ready to explode" and that he needed me. He wanted to have sex. I hesitated because I didn't really feel ready for that. He got kind of mad and said I had made him so hard and that I needed to "finish what I started" and that it wasn't fair of me to leave him with "blue balls" because it would be painful. I felt kind of scared and just kind of mumbled that I was really sorry but I had to go. I got out of there really quickly and stayed away from him after that. Later I learned that if I had slept with him that could have been considered rape, because he was pressuring me. My therapist told me that it is never too late to change your mind about sex, and that it's okay to leave someone with an erection even if it's really uncomfortable for them. She also said there is no such thing as "blue balls"—he could have just masturbated or waited it out and the erection would just go away.

People are sometimes confused about what counts as rape. I want to give a few examples and clarifications, though they may be triggering to some people.

- If you orgasm while being raped, it doesn't mean you "wanted it" or that it wasn't rape.
- It doesn't have to hurt to be rape, though it often does.
- It is rape if you were sleeping when someone penetrated your vagina.
- It is still rape if you were both drunk, as you being drunk means you could not give consent.
- It is still rape if you are dating the person who raped you. In fact, most rapes are acquaintance rapes, not random strangers.
- Rape happens to people of all genders, not just to people with vaginas.

Sexual abuse

If a teacher, doctor, family member, boss, or anyone much older than you does anything sexual to you as a child, that is sexual abuse. Sexual abuse also includes sexual activity performed on anyone unable to give consent. It is important to tell a safe and trusted adult as soon as possible if this is happening.

I have heard from people who were scared to report anything because they didn't want to get in trouble. The fault is never on the child for sexual abuse, even if they agreed to it or kept the secret for a long time.

♥ Everyone in my junior year English class thought our teacher was really hot. He was only 24, and we were all 16 and 17. I found myself being extra giggly and even occasionally flirting when I stayed after class to talk to him. When he started flirting back, though, I felt sick to my stomach and started being terrified of going to school. I told some of my friends, but they just congratulated me for having such a hot guy interested in me. I couldn't tell my parents, either, because I was terrified they'd bring it up to the school and my teacher would tell them how I'd "started it." I felt like a bad person for having ever flirted with him in the first place. I texted a crisis hotline one time because I couldn't stop thinking about it, and the person really helped me to forgive myself. She said it was totally natural for me to be flirtatious as a teen, and that there was no excuse for him flirting back with me. I just avoided him for the rest of the year, but sometimes I still feel icky thinking about it. It's weird how someone just flirting with you can make you feel violated.

What should I do if I have been assaulted or raped?

The most important thing is to get somewhere safe. Go somewhere crowded or find help.

Even if you have no idea what you want to do, or if you want to press charges, going to a hospital for a rape kit can keep your options open. Don't change your clothes or wash yourself off—go straight to the hospital, clinic, or police station.

Not only will you be able to have any possible evidence collected, but seeing a doctor afterwards allows you to be provided with care. You might want to take an emergency contraceptive, test for STIs, and get medicine to prevent **HIV (human immunodeficiency virus)**. The doctor or nurse can also examine you for injuries, such as tearing of the vagina or anus.

Sometimes, people are not aware that they were raped and/or assaulted. They may have been drugged (quick tip—never accept an open drink from anyone unless you are 100 percent sure it is safe!), or they may not have consented but be confused because the person they were with was either a friend or a partner. Sometimes people just feel violated or upset after having what they thought was sex, and they really don't know why they feel that way. If you think you may have been assaulted or raped, find a trusted and knowledgeable adult to discuss it with. Remember the FRIES rule for consent; all five elements are needed for it to be consensual sex.

Content warning: Assault story

♥ When I was 15, I spent a summer with a bunch of cousins. I got really close to this one cousin, a first cousin of mine, and we would spend all day and night together. He was a few years older than me, so I felt so cool that we were tight. We'd sleep with all the cousins spread out in sleeping bags all across the family room, and I'd always sleep hugging him. I really loved him, just like in a normal way.

One night though, I woke up really groggy and his hand was in my shirt. He wasn't touching my breasts, but he was hovering right above them. I was confused and asked what was happening and he asked if he could just feel them once. I said yes because I didn't really know what else to do. I can't believe I said yes, but I was so confused and sleepy and this was my cousin who I trusted so much. In the morning, I felt even more confused and also really gross and violated and sad. For some reason though, I kept acting like nothing happened and so did he. We even still hung out together and he slept next to me and we'd share headphones and listen to music. He'd secretly hold my hand sometimes at dinner. I felt gross and it all felt wrong but at the same time I didn't want to cause any trouble. Nothing else happened, and I didn't tell anyone for years. One day I finally told my sister, and she said something similar had happened with her a different year. I felt assaulted but I had said yes, so I didn't really know what to think. Only now do I know that my consent was not freely given or enthusiastic. I don't think I'll ever think about him or that night without feeling freshly violated. I get triggered by the most random things, like songs we both liked or even just thinking about visiting the country he lives in.

Decide if you want to file a police report. If you do, it is a good idea to have someone there to support you and advocate for you. Many sexual assault service providers, like RAINN, have people who will accompany you to the hospital or police station. Some people are hesitant because they understandably don't want to deal with the emotions the experience can create and would rather try to forget and move on. Some people are scared or anxious to go to the police. Remember first and foremost that you did nothing wrong. It can be frustrating to try to pursue justice, as many cases do get dropped for lack of evidence. But having a police report on file can still potentially help someone in the future making a case against your assailant. In some cases, you could also request a restraining order be placed on the person.

Seek therapy or support groups to talk about your experience. It can be hard to feel safe again after feeling violated in this way, and it is often helpful to see you are not alone and to talk about your experiences. Therapy or support groups can also help remind you that it was *not* your fault. It doesn't matter what you were wearing, how much you drank, or if you initiated sexual activity. Sexual harassment, assault, abuse, and rape are never the fault of the person assaulted.

Therapy may also be important in order to help you trust someone again in a future relationship. People who have been hurt in previous relationships often find it more difficult to trust in future ones.

Anonymous sex ed question box

"Is it okay to be scared of sex after being raped?"

Absolutely, this is normal. I'm so sorry if this has happened to you. If you have therapy resources available to you, please use them. It is important to process your trauma in order to heal. There are also free online, phone, and text resources you can use to find someone to talk to. Don't feel rushed or pressured to have sex again. Let your partner know that you may be triggered by certain things, and that you are not sure when and if you'll be ready for sex or how you will react to it.

"I had sex with my boyfriend when we were both drunk, but I wasn't really ready to have sex yet. I didn't do much, but I didn't say no. My friend says that counts as rape but it was my boyfriend and he was drunk too. I'm really confused and I feel kind of gross I guess, mostly because I don't want to think of him as raping me."

This is a really tricky situation, but I first just want to say I am so sorry this happened to you. I understand how confusing it must feel, especially if you don't think your boyfriend meant to do anything harmful to you. **If you were drunk, you were not able to give consent**, even to your boyfriend. So yes, this could be considered rape. However, I also understand that part of feeling "gross" might be that you don't want to consider your first time having "sex" with your boyfriend as rape, and perhaps it doesn't feel that way. I honestly think this is a really difficult situation and it is okay for you to process it however feels right to you. Trust your instincts, and talk to some trusted adults or use the resources in this book to find support.

"My friend is really nervous around her uncle because he is kind of inappropriate with her. But he hasn't actually done anything, he just touches her in ways that make her feel uncomfortable. I don't know how to help her."

I'm really glad you are looking out for your friend. This kind of thing is too common, and people are often confused about how to handle these situations because they involve a family member, and they don't want to make things "uncomfortable" by speaking up. But your friend has the right to feel safe. You could encourage her to say something to her parents about it. If she doesn't want to, however, don't pressure her. It is her choice. Just help by listening to her and helping her make a plan to stay safe, such as not being alone with her uncle. You could also encourage her to use one of the resources in the back of the book to talk to a trained adult.

Chapter 4

Safer Sex
(It Doesn't Kill the Mood)

An extremely important part of learning about sex is learning about how to have safer sex. Having a healthy sex life means being responsible about any potential physical consequences of sexual activity. These can be classified into two categories: sexually transmitted infections/diseases and pregnancy.

STIs/STDs

First of all, people use these two terms interchangeably, but there is a difference between them. A sexually transmitted infection is any infection you get from sexual contact. This includes any activity where the genitals and/or your mouth come in contact with another's genitals and/or mouth. A sexually transmitted disease is when the infection becomes symptomatic. Really the only difference is if you have symptoms, that becomes an STD. There are other ways to get some STIs, which are transferred through blood; the most common other way to contract one of these infections is by sharing needles (for example, when using drugs).

Some common STIs/STDs (with notes from the CDC (Centers for Disease Control and Prevention) website):

Chlamydia: common, treatable. If left undetected and untreated, it can make it hard to get pregnant later in life.

Gonorrhea: common, treatable. If left untreated can cause very serious health complications.

Hepatitis: affects the liver and is the leading cause of liver cancer.

Herpes: common, often undiagnosed. Many people don't realize they have it. Not curable, but there are medicines to reduce outbreaks and transmission.

HIV/AIDS: human immunodeficiency virus/acquired immunodeficiency syndrome. More on this below.

HPV: human papillomavirus. The most common STI in the United States. Can cause various cancers. It has a vaccine available to teens that is recommended highly by the American Academy of Pediatrics.

PID: pelvic inflammatory disease. Can lead to serious consequences, including infertility.

Syphilis: very easy to cure with the right treatment; extremely serious health consequences if left untreated.

There is no foolproof way to avoid an STI other than complete lack of sexual contact. STIs can be mostly prevented, however, by the use of barrier methods, such as condoms, dental dams, and medical grade gloves. Make sure you are using protection that is not old or expired, so that it does not degrade or rip. Condoms should be well fitted so they don't slip off during sex. Keep condoms away from heat, and don't use anything sharp to open a condom wrapper. Condoms are extremely important for protection against STIs and unwanted pregnancy.

♥ I still remember once my boyfriend and I were having sex and I pulled out a condom I had bought at the store. This was my first time buying them and I thought I'd stroke his ego by buying an extra-large sized one to let him know I was impressed, you know? Well, we used the condom, and after he came, he went to remove it and couldn't find it. It had slipped off inside my vajayjay! Luckily the ring thing was still near the surface and I could grab it and pull it out, but I was so scared I'd get an STD or get pregnant. I guess condoms are definitely *not* one size fits all.

A condom made for use inside a vagina is called an **internal condom**. Internal condoms are placed inside the vagina instead of on the penis. These, too, can help protect against STIs as well as pregnancy. Dental dams are used for oral sex, to create a barrier between the mouth and genitals. Some people use gloves to protect themselves from unintentional transfer of fluids during contact with the genitals, including the penis, vagina, and anus. There is something known as a finger condom that could be used instead of latex gloves, but these are more likely to fall off during sexual activity.

Other ways to prevent yourself from getting or transmitting STIs include regular testing for yourself and partners, as well as strong communication within your relationship. Have a conversation about the importance of staying safe and your expectations for monogamy. If you are sexually active, you should be tested for STIs at least once a year. If you have more than one partner, share needles, or don't use protection each time you have sex, you should be tested every three to six months.

HIV

HIV is a sexually transmitted infection that I think deserves its own section. There is a lot of stigma around HIV/AIDS, which started when I was growing up and still perpetuates today. In the 1980s and 1990s, the images of HIV and AIDS were often misleading, and there was a lot of fear. People did not know how it was transmitted and isolated themselves from anyone with AIDS for fear of it being contagious. Being gay was also less well accepted than it is now, so there was a lot of blame put on people with AIDS, who were disproportionately gay men, for their "lifestyle choices."

The problem with this stigma is that it socially isolates people who, just like the rest of us, need our support. It leads to mental health issues and can create internalized feelings of shame or despair. It also is based on misleading assumptions about HIV.

HIV is an initialism for human immunodeficiency virus. It is a virus that weakens the immune system. It does this by destroying cells that are needed to fight infection. If not treated, it can become AIDS. The difference between HIV and AIDS is that AIDS is the most serious stage of an HIV infection. AIDS is what happens when the virus destroys too many T cells, or CD4 cells, in your body.

HIV is transmitted through vaginal and anal sex, sharing needles or syringes (drugs, tattoos, piercings), and by getting bodily fluids, including blood, semen, or vaginal fluids, into an open cut. HIV can also be passed from a mother to child during childbirth, but there is a medicine that reduces the risk.

HIV isn't spread through saliva, so you can't get HIV from kissing or sharing food or drink. HIV isn't spread through casual contact, like holding hands or hugging. It used to be true that HIV could be acquired from a blood transfusion, but that is no longer the case, due to improvements in screening and testing of donated blood.

♥ I remember when I first met my friend Jax, it was senior year of college. He seemed cool so I asked him if he wanted to grab coffee with me and work on an assignment together. We talked for hours, and eventually he shared that he was HIV positive. I told him how sorry I was and gave him a hug. I didn't expect him to respond so strongly, but he gave me a fierce hug back, and when we separated he had tears in his eyes. He said when people found out about him, they usually got really awkward and stepped backwards as if they were going to "catch AIDS" just by standing too close. He had gotten so used to being treated like an untouchable that my hug and acceptance of him was almost more than he could handle in that moment. Jax and I stayed friends a long time, until he passed away a few years ago. I'll never forget what a difference a little love and understanding can make.

There is a daily medicine you can take to help prevent HIV if you are at higher risk, called PrEP (pre-exposure prophylaxis). If you think that is something you would benefit from, you can talk to your doctor about it. Anyone who has casual, unprotected sex should speak to their doctor about PrEP.

HIV is not curable, but it is treatable, especially if caught early. There are even post-exposure prophylactics (PEP) that can help if taken immediately after exposure. That's why it is so important to get tested and be educated on how to stay safer. Treatment can help you live a longer and healthier life.

Pregnancy

The other major physical consequence of sexual activity is the potential for pregnancy. You can get pregnant from penis-in-vagina sex, which allows for semen, carrying sperm, to exit the penis and enter the vagina. From there, the sperm travels up through the uterus. If it comes in contact with an egg from the ovaries, the sperm can fertilize the egg. That egg can implant itself in the uterine lining and grow into a baby.

The problem is, we are biologically capable of making a baby long before we are actually ready to have a baby. Most people are not emotionally, mentally, and financially stable enough to carry and raise a baby while they are still in their tweens and teens, and many people are not even ready in their twenties or thirties. Our bodies, however, are capable of getting pregnant from early puberty. While there are options for ending a pregnancy in many locations (see the section on abortion below), it is still best for your emotional and physical health to use birth control methods, which can help you reduce the chance of becoming pregnant.

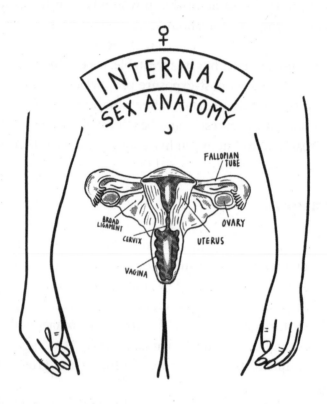

If you think you might be pregnant, a home pregnancy test can usually detect a pregnancy immediately after your first missed period. Some can even test a few days before. You can't test for pregnancy immediately after sex—it takes time for the hormone levels to change.

Remember that birth control methods *do not* necessarily protect against STIs! The only ones that do are condoms. All other methods of birth control protect against pregnancy but *not* STIs.

Some methods of birth control include:

- **implant**
  - → a small, rod-like device that is implanted in your arm
  - → 99 percent effective and lasts up to five years
  - → works by giving your body progestin, which thickens the cervix
  - → stops sperm from entering the uterus, and may stop eggs from being released

- **IUD (intrauterine device)**
  - → a small, T-shaped piece of flexible plastic placed into your uterus
  - → either hormonal or copper
  - → hormonal IUDs use progestin as well, and last three to seven years depending on the brand
  - → copper IUDs work because sperm doesn't like copper, so it stops sperm from entering the uterus
  - → 99 percent effective
  - → do not use with a menstrual cup

- **shot**
  - → 94 percent effective
  - → repeat every three months
  - → also uses progestin
  - → might need to wait a week for it to be effective

- **pill**
  - → 91 percent effective in practice (99 percent if used perfectly, but people miss pills, which reduces the effectiveness rate a lot)
  - → take a daily pill
  - → uses estrogen and progestin or progestin only
  - → combination helps stop ovulation; progestin only thickens cervical mucus

- **patch**
  - → 91 percent effective
  - → needs to be changed on schedule
  - → uses two hormones, progestin and estrogen
  - → the additional hormones in the patch stop ovulation completely
  - → estrogen is not advised for smokers, people with migraines with aura, heart conditions, blood pressure issues, diabetes, blood disorders, and breast cancer—it's important to talk to a doctor about the risks for you

- **condoms**
  - → 85 percent effective
  - → wear on the penis to prevent semen from entering the vagina
  - → must be used properly every time

- **internal condoms**
  - → 79 percent effective
  - → wear inside the vagina to prevent semen from entering the uterus
  - → must be used properly every time

- **sterilization**
  - → later in life, when you are sure you don't want a baby, there are surgical procedures that can stop sperm from entering your ejaculate or stop eggs from reaching the uterus

- **male birth control pill**
  - → not yet available—in the research phase
  - → works by stopping the production of sperm

→ allows AMABs even more control over preventing unwanted pregnancy vs. condoms alone

If you have unprotected sex, in many areas you can access
an emergency contraceptive (sometimes called the "morning-
after pill") to reduce your chances of becoming pregnant. The
most well-known emergency contraceptive is called Plan B.
A less easy to access but super effective (99 percent) form of
emergency protection is to get an IUD inserted within five
days of having unprotected sex.

All of these can help prevent pregnancy, but none of
them are 100 percent effective. While it is unlikely, it is still
possible for you to get pregnant while both taking the pill
AND using a condom. That is a risk you are accepting when
you choose to have sex. This risk is higher if you don't use
birth control and protection correctly every single time—for
example, if you miss a pill, let a condom rip, or place it on
too loosely. You can get pregnant at any point in your cycle,
including while on your period. You can also get pregnant
if you are taking testosterone hormones; they do not work
as a contraceptive.

On the flip side, if you *want* to get pregnant, then it is
important that you still protect yourself from STIs. This
can be tricky, since the methods to protect you from STIs
typically are also meant to protect against pregnancy. If you
are with a long-term, monogamous partner, you should both
get tested for STIs, and then you could stop using any form
of protection in order to get pregnant.

I believe it is the responsibility of both partners equally
to protect against pregnancy during sex. It is common for
someone to feel pressured to let their partner not use a condom. Remember that health, safety, and comfort are just as

important, and that the use of a condom doesn't necessarily reduce pleasure. While condoms do change the physical contact, there are a large variety of condoms and lubes available, including ones with textures and ribbing, that are meant to increase pleasure.

♥ My boyfriend keeps pressuring me to not use a condom, since he says it feels so much better that way. I do get that it's more fun and feels better sometimes to not wear a condom...but also, it's not at all worth the risk of me getting pregnant. He says that I should just take the pill or use an IUD, but I don't want to risk getting an STI. Now, he's really upset because he says I don't trust him enough, and I don't know what to do. I do think it's a red flag that he keeps pressuring me, so I might have to break up with him if he doesn't let us use a condom.

Condoms and internal condoms

Condoms are thin, stretchy barriers you can use on a penis or internally in a vagina. Both external and internal condoms work the same way—by preventing the sperm from reaching the uterus. With an external condom, you pinch a very small bit of the end and hold that at the tip of the penis. You then unroll the condom back over the penis until it ends near the base.

To use an internal condom, you pinch the inner ring and insert it into your vagina. You then use your finger to push the condom back into place, with the outer ring sitting just outside the vulva. During sex, you can hold the outer ring in place to prevent it from sliding. After, twist the top and pull the condom out to dispose of it.

Adoption

Despite all of the various protection methods available, people do still end up pregnant and unready to raise a baby. I am sorry if you end up in this situation; I know it is a very emotional position to be in. There is a lot to consider if you end up pregnant, or if you end up impregnating someone else. If you are young, there is your education, financial stability, support system, and mental health to consider, as well as the best interests of your future child. I hope you have trusted adults in your life to talk the decision over with; but if you don't, there are many resources (see the back of the book) available to help support you.

One option in this situation is to carry your baby to term and then put your baby up for **adoption**. Putting your baby up for adoption means giving up parental rights to your child. If you are pregnant but feel unfit to take care of a baby, adoption is a way for you to try to provide that child with the life you want it to have. Choosing adoption means you will still need to disrupt your life for nine months while you carry the baby to term. You will need to handle any medical complications of your pregnancy; deal with body aches, pains, and nausea; avoid food, drinks, and activities that are bad for the baby; and make regular visits to a doctor for prenatal care. Choosing to stay pregnant as a teenager decreases your chances of academic success, with only 50 percent of teen mothers receiving a high school diploma by age 22. You will also need to deal with the potential trauma of carrying a baby inside of you for months and then having to give it up.

Despite these difficulties, some teens do choose to stay pregnant and give their child up for adoption. This is usually due to ethical concerns with abortion, either from themself, their partner, their religious leadership, or family members. If this is what you choose, there are many private adoption companies you can work with. Hospitals also often have contacts you can call if you decide on adoption during labor and need an immediate home for your child.

It may help emotionally when choosing to give a baby up for adoption to know that children of teen parents are more likely to have lower school achievement and to drop out of high school. According to the CDC, they have more health problems and are more likely to serve jail time at some time during adolescence, to give birth as a teenager, and to face unemployment as a young adult.

Abortion

To have an **abortion** means to purposely end a pregnancy, either in a clinic or by using an abortion pill. This is not an easy decision for most people, but some people do see it as the best option. Abortions are not available legally everywhere, so you'll need to check with your state's or country's laws to know what options you have.

The abortion pill works until 11 weeks of pregnancy, and it can often be taken at home. The abortion pill is made up of two different medications: mifepristone and misoprostol. Mifepristone stops your body from producing progesterone, which stops the fetus from growing. The second medicine, misoprostol, causes cramping and bleeding to empty your uterus. It's like having a really heavy period. The pill is not 100 percent effective. Depending on how early in your pregnancy you take it, and if you take a second dose, it is anywhere from 87 to 99 percent effective. Some people do end up having an in-clinic abortion after taking the pill if it doesn't work.

If you have an abortion in a clinic, it is a procedure that works by using suction. If you are further along in the pregnancy, you may need a dilation and evacuation (D&E), which uses suction along with medical tools. In-clinic abortions are extremely effective, almost 100 percent.

Some places allow abortions for a limited timeframe (up until a certain week of pregnancy)...others don't allow abortions at all. The laws are changing constantly, with really strong opinions on all sides. Some common terms people use to describe their beliefs around abortion are **pro-life** and **pro-choice**. Even these terms are contentious, and not everyone defines them in the same way.

Pro-life refers to someone who believes abortion is morally wrong. This may be for personal, cultural, or religious reasons. Some people who are pro-life believe abortion is always wrong, but many believe there are cases where it is okay, such as if the pregnancy is putting the mother's life at risk. Some people who call themselves pro-life will also allow a pregnancy to be terminated if it was caused by rape or abuse. Pro-life people believe that a fetus is a baby, and that aborting a fetus would be murder. They argue that if a person chose to have sex, they should accept the consequences of their actions.

Pro-choice refers to someone who believes that abortion decisions should be the choice of the person who is pregnant. They believe that since it is that person's body, the decision should be between them and perhaps their doctor. They believe that the person who is pregnant has the right to make the best choice for their body and for their own life.

There are a lot of people whose beliefs don't fall squarely into one of these two categories. Some people, for example, are morally opposed to abortion, but still believe that abortion should be legal for other reasons. This group often pushes to keep abortion legal but to decrease the need for abortion through better sex education for all. The focus is then on preventing an unwanted pregnancy from happening in the first place.

One reason a person may want abortion to be legal is because it is known what happens when abortions are made illegal. We have examples from the past when abortions were illegal in the United States. They still happened, but since they had to be done in secret, they happened in inhumane and unsafe conditions. Another reason some people support legal abortion is the lack of public support structures for living with an unwanted pregnancy and handling adoption procedures.

Abortion is not an easy decision, with lots to consider. Just know that you are not alone in struggling with this, and there are people you can talk to if you need support.

♥ My entire family is very religious and would probably disown me if I ever got visibly pregnant. Abortion is also illegal in my religion, so I really had no idea what to do when I had unprotected sex one time. The next morning, I rushed to my local Planned Parenthood and bought Plan B. I'm lucky that I took it immediately, otherwise the chances of it being effective would have been a lot lower. I didn't feel like I was doing anything wrong by using Plan B, because a pregnancy hadn't even formed yet. If I had gotten pregnant, I really don't know what options I would even have had. I'd have to choose between being disowned by my family and committing a sin that I might never be able to forgive myself for. I just wish I had used protection to begin with; I'll never make that mistake again.

Anonymous sex ed question box

"I think I'm pregnant. I did it with my bf and I haven't told anyone yet and I don't know how."

There are a few things to consider here. First of all, there are readily available pregnancy tests in most areas, ones that you can use at home. It would be really helpful to know if pregnancy is a real concern. If you have someone trusted to go with you, the support could be nice. If you had unprotected sex, it's also really important to go get tested for STIs. You can do this at a clinic or with your doctor.

If you are pregnant, it can be beneficial to find a trusted friend or family member to talk to about your options. Let them know that you understand you may have made a mistake but that you really need them to be there to support you rather than lecture you. If you don't want to tell anyone, you can talk to a doctor anonymously, go to a clinic, or try some of the hotlines listed in our resources.

"Can a condom get stuck inside a vagina?"

Yes, it's possible. Sometimes a condom can slip off during sex, often because it is either too big or too small, or if it isn't removed promptly after ejaculating. Since the vagina has a cervix at the top, the condom really can't go too far in. Often, you can get it back out just by hooking it out with clean fingers. If it is out of your reach, you could head to a clinic or doctor's office if need be. Do not insert anything into your vagina to pull it out other than your fingers!

If this happens, you'll need to consider the possibility of semen having leaked out. This means increased risk for STIs and for pregnancy. You can reduce your risk by taking an emergency contraceptive, and you should get tested for STIs.

"Can you start having sex raw and put on a condom after?"

If you start having sex without a condom, you are not protected against STIs. While this might offer some amount of protection from pregnancy, it will not protect you the same amount as wearing a condom properly the entire time. It is possible to get pregnant from precum, the small amount of ejaculation that is released for lubrication before orgasm. It is also possibly less pleasurable to stop to put on a condom once you have momentum going.

"How can sex feel as good with a condom on as it feels without one?"

Sex is not just the feeling of the penis inside the vagina. For most people, a large part of the enjoyment is in the connection between partners and in the pleasure you are providing and receiving. Knowing that you are helping your partner and yourself to be safe can make sex more relaxing, reducing stress on both partners. There are many types of condoms on the market that help increase sensation. There are ultra-thin ones, ones with special lubricants to increase intensity, and ones with textured ribs.

"How does a condom break?"

A condom can break by getting a tear in it. This typically happens if the condom is too old, making the material wear down, or if it has been mishandled. Many people keep condoms in their wallet, but that actually keeps it too close to their body, which might make it too warm. It's a tradeoff, as having it in your wallet also makes it more likely that you will have one on hand when you need it! Condoms can also tear from using something sharp to open the packet, like your teeth, or from getting snagged on something while putting it on.

"Do you need to use a condom every time?"

If you want to protect against STI and/or pregnancy, then yes. Every single time, and put it on properly.

"Are there times you don't have to use a condom?"

If you are in a long-term, monogamous relationship and have both been tested for STIs, it is possible that birth control alone is enough protection for you. That is a personal decision based on your trust level and risk tolerance.

"What if I'm allergic to latex?"

There are non-latex condoms on the market, and the internal condom that can be used inside a vagina is not latex based.

"Can you get pregnant if you have sex in water and don't use a condom?"

Yes. Having sex under water does not change your ability to become pregnant.

"Do I use a condom for oral sex?"

Many people use something called a dental dam for oral sex. It is similar in concept to a condom, but it goes on the mouth instead of on a penis.

"What should I do if the condom breaks?"

If the condom breaks, you should consider emergency contraception. You should also both be tested for STIs.

"Can you use just a condom and not the pill?"

The condom by itself is only 85 percent effective against pregnancy. Most people prefer the 99 percent protection of an additional birth control method.

"Does a condom hurt?"

No, if used properly a condom should cause no pain to either partner.

"What kind of lube do I use with a condom?"

The important thing when using a condom is not to use an oil-based lubricant. Oil can break down the material of the condom, making it ineffective. Water- and silicone-based lubricants are safe to use with condoms.

"What is the point if they aren't 100 percent effective?"

Not using a condom gives you zero percent protection, and using one gives you 85 percent protection. So even if it is not a guarantee, it still provides a much lower chance of getting pregnant if you use a condom.

"How do you make it so that putting on the condom doesn't kill the mood?"

Putting on a condom really only takes a minute, and often it is done between foreplay and penetration. That means both partners are probably pretty turned on, and a short breather is not likely to kill the mood. Especially if you both have communicated ahead of time that you plan to use a condom, so that the pause is expected. While one person puts the condom on, the other can always continue with other sexual activity directed elsewhere on the body.

Chapter 5

Gender

(Hint: There Are More than Two)

ender is what our society believes it *means* to be a man or woman. This includes but is not limited to expected behaviors, roles, and norms. *Gender is not your biological sex traits.* Not every man or woman fits into these gender norms, but we do grow up surrounded by gendered language and expectations. For example, many boys are given more leeway to be physically rowdy and independent, and many girls are able to get away with misbehaving discreetly because they are assumed to be "sweet." Boys are told not to cry, and girls are expected to need comfort. In some cultures, boys are pushed toward certain future jobs and girls toward others. This starts with having girls do more household chores and boys do more outside chores (such as lawn mowing or helping fix up a car).

Even our toys are more gendered now than they used to be, with companies like LEGO® selling pink doggy day care and ice cream stand toys that are clearly marketed toward girls. Dads often will take only their boys fishing; moms will take only their girls to the spa. Boys are often called "assertive" when behaving the same way that gets girls scolded for being "bossy." Gender is a concept we have made up as a society—which means it is also something we can reinvent as a society.

Some people don't fit into the norm that society has created but still feel comfortable identifying as a girl or boy (woman or man). If looking for a label, they might fit into a category called **gender nonconforming**. This simply means choosing to not dress or act in the way society expects. A gender nonconforming boy, for example, might wear makeup, nail polish, or skirts; grow their hair long; or go into traditionally female-dominated professions. They are still a cisgender boy, but they go against societal expectations.

Cisgender means having the same **gender identity** as assumed based on your biological sex (this describes the majority of people); it is the opposite of transgender.

Some people feel that the gender they were assigned at birth is wrong. They may feel gender dysphoria, like perhaps parts of their body don't fit who they are. **Dysphoria** is significant distress related to a strong desire to be another gender, which may include the desire to change physical parts of your body to match societal expectations. Many trans people assigned female at birth, for example, experience dysphoria at times over their breasts, or wish they had a penis.

The opposite of dysphoria is **gender euphoria**, a feeling of joy about one's gender expression and presentation. Dysphoria can be very difficult emotionally, but it can help to know that once properly addressed, a person can experience euphoria about their outward gender appearance. This is also true for those without dysphoria.

★ Summer, one of my younger teens, came out two years ago as nonbinary. They started using they/them pronouns and seemed much happier that they were no longer treated as a "boy." They still dealt with a significant amount of depression over the next couple of years and often couldn't place the root cause. Recently, Summer came out again as a transgender girl. She is now using she/they pronouns and completely stopped using her birth name. To surprise her and show my support, I went shopping and bought her some feminine-presenting clothes. I thought they might help her feel more like a "girl" in society. It was a total joy watching her try them on. She was so happy and flapping her arms (an autism stim). She wanted photos taken for the first time ever in her life that I can remember. It was amazing to see how much joy and euphoria she felt over the person she saw reflected back in the mirror.

If you are born into what is assumed to be a boy's body, but your gender identity is a girl—or vice versa—then you are **transgender**. This means your gender identity doesn't match the gender you were assigned at birth. This is now sometimes called "binary transgender," because you are still one of the two binary genders: man or woman, boy or girl.

Recently, we have developed a new term to describe those who are **nonbinary**, meaning their gender doesn't fit either of the two binary genders. Nonbinary is not just one gender identity; it includes many different gender identities outside of woman and man.

Being nonbinary is not a new experience; there just wasn't a common term for it for a long time. Indigenous people have a term, "two spirit," which encompasses genders outside of the binary, and in Hawaii there is a similar term, māhū. In these cultures, nonbinary people were given important spiritual and social roles. Colonization erased much of this rich history, but people are starting to reclaim it within their cultural practices.

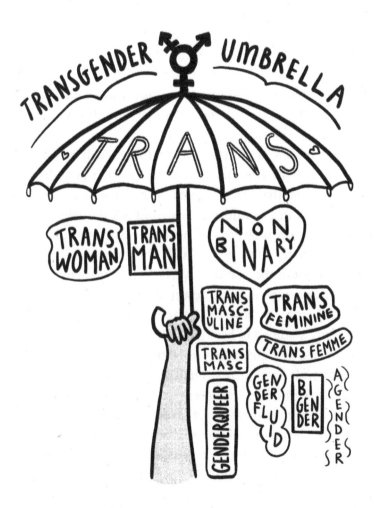

Biological sex vs. gender identity

One way people like to troll our Normalizers TikTok account is by declaring, "there's only two genders" or "ur a girl." They say this knowing that Asha, as a nonbinary teen, feels **misgendered** by these statements. The idea of someone being nonbinary, neither woman nor man, has caused a lot of animosity on social media and in real life as well. I think this harassment, like most forms of hate, is due to a lack of understanding and education. Many people are uncomfortable with or feel threatened by change. I hope reading this chapter will help people better understand the nonbinary and trans community.

Biological sex is the physical anatomy (such as genitals), chromosomes (X and Y), and hormones (such as androgens and estrogens) that you are born with. There are a number of variations in chromosomes beyond XX (female) and XY (male). Your chromosomes help dictate how your body develops. **Intersex** refers to people with chromosomal variations. There are a number of such variations, and many people have variations that go undetected because their anatomy still develops in an expected manner. These people might be mistakenly assumed to have XX or XY chromosomes and still be identified as a girl or boy at birth.

Your gender assigned at birth is the gender identity that you are assumed to be based on your physical features. If you are assigned male at birth, you are likely to be raised in society as a boy, with all the gender norms and expectations our society has decided are *normal* for boys. Your "gender assigned at birth" would be a boy, which may or may not match how you feel about your gender inside.

Gender identity is the gender you identify with; it's who

you feel you are inside. You don't have to change a single thing about your outside self to match your gender identity. If you feel your identity is a girl, you can look and live exactly like society's expectations of a boy and still be a girl inside. You would still be a girl in your thoughts and feelings and perceptions of the world.

Transgender means someone's gender identity is different from their biological sex. This can include binary transgender as well as nonbinary identities. Someone who is transgender should be treated as their gender identity, no matter whether or not they have **transitioned**. If someone does not have their gender identity validated, it can create increased feelings of dysphoria. Dysphoria can lead to depression, and can manifest as eating disorders, anxiety, and even suicidality. If you struggle with these, you can find resources in the back of this book that can help you to get the support you need.

Gender expression

Gender expression is how we show off our gender to the outside world. Gender expression includes how we dress and our hairstyle, makeup choices, name, pronouns, and mannerisms. It can also include medically altering our physical anatomy or hormones. You can't look at someone's gender expression and assume you know their gender identity.

A girl can have short hair and dress in a way deemed to be masculine; a boy can wear a dress and still be a boy. Our gender expression doesn't define our identity. If you dress like a "girl" but are born a "boy," that doesn't *make* you transgender. Someone who is gender nonconforming may still be the same gender they were assumed at birth.

Nonbinary people also don't have to follow any one particular gender expression. Nonbinary people can look fully feminine, masculine, androgynous (gender neutral), or anything in between.

Nonbinary people can also use any pronouns, including the ones that typically match their assigned sex at birth. Many nonbinary people have begun using they/them pronouns, using "they" in its singular form. For example, I would say, "Asha went out to the market, but they will be home soon."

♥ Every story I read about transmasculine people says something like, "Ever since I was two, I felt different." But honestly, I don't think I behaved any differently from the other girls. Sure, I was a bit more masculine and brash, but I still liked skirts and I still liked makeup (I do even now!). But at the same time, the label "woman" doesn't feel right for me at all, and I strongly prefer they/them, he/him, and xe/xem pronouns. I didn't come out until recently, in my mid-twenties, and nobody's taking me seriously since I never behaved particularly masculine. It really hurts to hear all the misgendering and to know that nobody believes me. I'm starting to wonder if I'm wrong in transitioning, but I know they/he/xe pronouns and androgynous terms are what make me happiest. And I know that I don't feel a connection to being a woman.

Social transitioning

Changing parts of your gender expression to match your gender identity is called "transitioning." There are various forms of transitioning, in both social and medical ways. It is important to note that transitioning is *not* in any way required in order to be transgender.

Social transitioning is changing the surface ways in which society perceives you. This could include changes to your name or the pronouns you ask people to use for you and changes to your clothing, makeup, and hairstyle. When people change their name, they often refer to their birth name as their **deadname**. This term means that the name causes them distress, dysphoria, or trauma, and they'd prefer not to hear it anymore.

Using the wrong pronouns for someone is called **misgendering**. Not all transgender people change their pronouns, and not everyone who changes their pronouns is transgender. It is respectful to ask someone their pronouns, as even if you think it's "clear" how to refer to a person, you may be unintentionally misgendering them. I view that as an opportunity to educate them! Sharing your own pronouns first is a simple way to do this.

Men typically use he/him pronouns, and women typically use she/her pronouns; however, anyone of any gender can use any pronouns based on what feels comfortable to them. When we don't know someone's gender, we use they/them for them in English. An example would be if an unknown person left their car keys on a coffee table, and you wanted to call attention to it. You might say it exactly like that: "Excuse me, someone left their car keys here!" You'd be referring to *one* person using *their*. We use they/them in both the singular and plural all the time, often without realizing it. Many nonbinary people enjoy the androgyny of using they/them pronouns, but not all nonbinary people use this pronoun set.

Just as anyone can use they/them pronouns, anyone can

also choose to use she/her or he/him pronouns. Typically, people use the pronouns that are associated with their gender identity, although some people may not feel safe doing so and may stick with pronouns that match their gender expression.

Some people choose to use newer pronoun sets, known as **neopronouns**. Some neopronouns are it/itself, zi/hir and xe/xem. People often use neopronouns to distance themselves further from the gender binary. Many people are beginning to use combinations of pronoun sets. For example, someone might use "she/they" or "they/it." What this means is that the person is comfortable with multiple sets of pronouns being used for them.

♥ I was born in a "female" body, one with a vagina. I knew very young that I didn't feel like a girl, not because of my clothes or anything, just because it just always felt wrong to me. I didn't feel like anyone's daughter or sister. When I was nine, I came out to my family as a boy. They accepted me for the most part, and they let me change my name legally. I started using he/him pronouns. After a while, though, that didn't feel right either. I didn't feel right as a boy or as a girl. That's when I realized I was nonbinary, when I was 16. I asked people to use they/them pronouns for me, and eventually I tried out it/itself pronouns. The "it" pronouns felt right almost immediately. It was a relief to find something that felt so completely nongendered. I picked a new name for myself when I was 17, and I prefer my new name and the "it" pronouns. Some of my family still uses my boy name and he pronouns, and it feels misgendering, but I don't have the energy to keep correcting them anymore, I guess. I don't like the feeling, though. I tell people I use it/they pronouns so that if someone is really uncomfortable with using "it," they have the option to use they. It was cool to find out that there are languages where everyone and everything is an "it" without any gendered pronouns at all. In Modern Persian (Farsi), the same pronoun is used for men, women, nonbinary people, and objects!

One other way people transition is to alter the appearance of their physical anatomy without surgery. People born with breasts can choose to bind (wear a binder) to reduce the appearance of their breasts. A binder is a piece of compression material similar to a sports bra but with much more compression.

Binders are mostly safe, but do come with risks, especially if not worn properly. Some of the ways people use binders incorrectly are by wearing them for too long (they should be worn for no more than six to eight hours per day), wearing them during exercise, sleeping in them, and wearing them too tight. You should be able to fit two fingers between your binder and your skin. Wearing a binder for a long period of time can cause some damage to your breast tissue and make top surgery (surgery to remove the breasts) more difficult. This is why it is important to let a medical professional know if you are binding and to follow binder safety rules. It is also important to weigh these risks against the mental health risks associated with your dysphoria. GC2B and Underworks are two reputable, high-quality chest binder retailers.

People born with a penis sometimes "tuck" their penis so that it appears flatter in the front. The gentlest way to tuck is to simply flatten back the penis and testicles and wear tighter underwear. Some people find this to be enough, while others use medical tape to help secure their penis. This method carries risk of irritation and makes using the bathroom more difficult. An even more extreme form of tucking involves carefully pushing the testicles back into the body somewhat. Discuss any of these methods with a medical professional if you are considering using them.

Some risks of tucking include urinary tract infections (UTIs), inflammation, twisting, and/or problems urinating. Untuck as often as you can, and do not tuck for long periods of time. If you use tape, be sure it is not too tight as to cut off blood circulation. Check for signs of skin irritation each time you tuck. Some alternatives to tucking include wearing a dance belt, which dancers use to reduce the appearance of a bulge, or simply wearing loose fitting clothing.

Medical transitioning

In addition to all of the above, some transgender individuals choose to medically transition. The simplest form of this is the use of puberty blockers. Puberty blockers are medicines that block testosterone and/or estrogen so that your body doesn't undergo the anticipated changes. Puberty blockers are reversible and are generally considered safe. They can have some side effects, which should be discussed carefully with your doctor. If you start on puberty blockers and then realize you are cisgender (the same gender as you were assigned at birth), you can simply stop the puberty blockers and your natural puberty will resume.

Rather than causing any permanent change to your body, puberty blockers simply put your body on pause. This allows you more time to carefully consider your identity. It is not safe to be on puberty blockers for longer than two years; by that point, doctors typically require patients to go off the blockers and resume their natural puberty, or to start hormone therapy. This allows the body to have the necessary hormones to protect bone health.

People use hormone therapies to medically transition their bodies. For example, someone AFAB might begin taking testosterone in order to deepen their voice, alter their genitals, and grow more body hair. This testosterone, if taken during puberty, will also continue the biological processes of puberty that their estrogen would have otherwise. Similarly, if an AMAB person uses puberty blockers to block their testosterone, they can eventually start taking estrogen to continue their puberty progression. They will develop breast buds and more feminine curves, and their penis will not grow into its natural full girth. This can, however, make it trickier to perform a vaginoplasty later if desired, as there is less penile tissue to use in the surgery.

There are a number of surgical procedures available to trans people in order to change their sexual anatomy. These are expensive but are life altering and potentially life saving for some individuals. These various procedures are known as top surgeries and bottom surgeries. Ideally, a person would work with a combination of doctors and psychologists to make sure this is the best option for them. In some locations, there are gender clinics with teams of medical professionals all working together to best support each person. Since these are permanent and riskier procedures, people usually wait until they are older to consider surgically altering their body. Some of the various gender-affirming surgeries include metoidioplasty, phalloplasty, and vaginoplasty. The diagrams on the following pages show how these surgeries are performed and are quite detailed, so feel free to skip past them unless they are of personal interest to you!

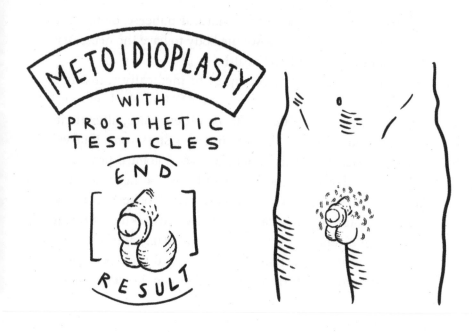

METOIDIOPLASTY

WITH

PROSTHETIC
TESTICLES

[END

RESULT]

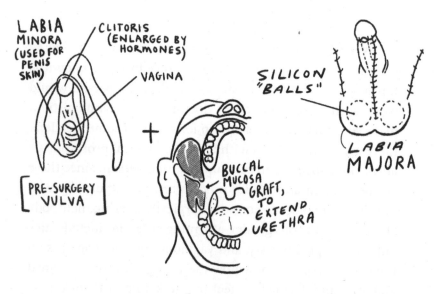

LABIA
MINORA
(USED FOR
PENIS
SKIN)

CLITORIS
(ENLARGED BY
HORMONES)

VAGINA

[PRE-SURGERY
VULVA]

+

BUCCAL
MUCOSA
GRAFT,
TO
EXTEND
URETHRA

SILICON
"BALLS"

LABIA
MAJORA

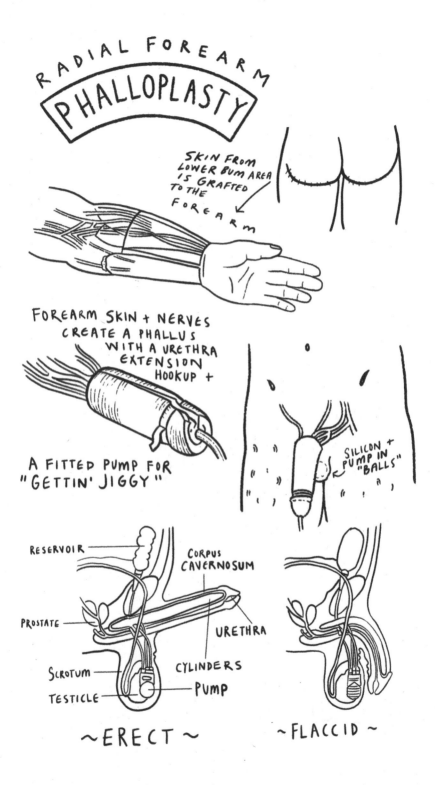

RADIAL FOREARM
PHALLOPLASTY

SKIN FROM LOWER BUM AREA IS GRAFTED TO THE FOREARM

FOREARM SKIN + NERVES CREATE A PHALLUS WITH A URETHRA EXTENSION HOOKUP +

A FITTED PUMP FOR "GETTIN' JIGGY"

SILICON + PUMP IN "BALLS"

RESERVOIR

CORPUS CAVERNOSUM

PROSTATE

URETHRA

SCROTUM

CYLINDERS

TESTICLE

PUMP

~ERECT~

~FLACCID~

VAGINOPLASTY

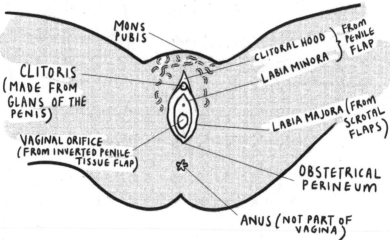

MONS PUBIS

CLITORAL HOOD } FROM PENILE FLAP

LABIA MINORA

CLITORIS (MADE FROM GLANS OF THE PENIS)

LABIA MAJORA (FROM SCROTAL FLAPS)

VAGINAL ORIFICE (FROM INVERTED PENILE TISSUE FLAP)

OBSTETRICAL PERINEUM

ANUS (NOT PART OF VAGINA)

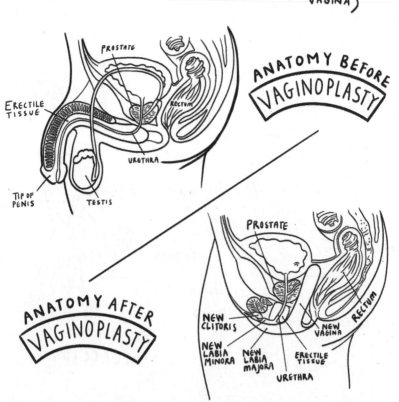

PROSTATE

ERECTILE TISSUE

RECTUM

URETHRA

TIP OF PENIS

TESTIS

ANATOMY BEFORE VAGINOPLASTY

PROSTATE

RECTUM

NEW CLITORIS

NEW VAGINA

NEW LABIA MINORA

NEW LABIA MAJORA

ERECTILE TISSUE

URETHRA

ANATOMY AFTER VAGINOPLASTY

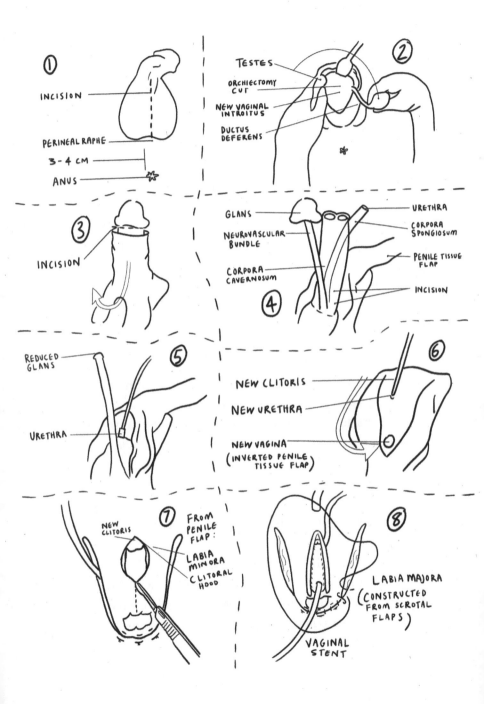

Some more identity terms

An "umbrella" label is one that encompasses other labels
within it. For example, transgender is a label that includes
both binary identities as well as nonbinary ones. Binary
transgender identities would simply be man or woman, but
opposite to a person's assigned gender at birth. Nonbinary
transgender identities include agender, bigender, demigender,
genderfluid, and others. More specific identity labels are
called "microlabels," and I will define some of these below.
Identity is complex and our use of these terms is still evolv-
ing. A label might mean one thing to one person and mean
something different to someone else. That's why conversation
about identity is so important.

★ One of my autistic teens, Mars, is nonbinary, and has always
disliked the gendering they come across in daily society.
They see it as unnecessary and exclusionary. Mars (it/they
pronouns) identifies as agender, meaning not identifying as
having any gender. Mars loves when people are confused
about its gender, because it helps Mars know that their outer
gender expression matches their internal gender identity.
"Confusing people gives me so much gender euphoria," says
Mars, usually with a large smile on its face.

Agender: not identifying as having any gender, genderless.

Autigender: autistic people often think about things logically,
which can lead to a disconnect with how many autistic people
view gender roles and norms. Many autistic people say that
society's views on gender don't make much sense. Someone

who is autigender believes that being autistic greatly impacts their relationship to gender.

Bigender: feeling like both boy and girl (man and woman) at the same time.

Demigirl/demiboy: having a partial but not complete attachment to one of the binary genders (girl or boy).

Genderfluid: a gender identity that changes gradually over time.

Gender neutral: having a preference for gender-neutral language and expectations.

Genderqueer: many people who use this label enjoy its ambiguity. It doesn't tell you much about the person other than that they are not cisgender.

Intersex: people born intersex have an atypical relationship to gender and sexuality because their anatomy, chromosomes, and/or hormones are not aligned to one binary sex. Sex assignment can often be murky in this case—for example, someone might be born with XX chromosomes and still produce androgens, causing them to have ambiguous genitals, such as an oversized clitoris and fused labia. Someone could be born with XY chromosomes and not be able to produce testosterone, causing them to be born with what appears to be a vagina.

There is a growing movement within the intersex community to not perform unnecessary medical procedures to make intersex babies externally match one of the binary biological sexes. In the past, people have opted to do sometimes risky and invasive surgeries on infants in order to "correct" their external genitalia and sex characteristics. The movement says it is not necessary to fit one of two binary genders and that it is cruel and unsafe to perform unnecessary medical procedures on infants.

Nonbinary: nonbinary is a different set of identities than binary transgender. Nonbinary people are not the complete opposite gender as assumed (female to male or vice versa). Nonbinary people find their identity is better described as something less concrete than girl/woman or boy/man. Nonbinary is not just a third gender label; it is a whole collection of identities.

Questioning: this is typically a temporary label that people use when they are questioning their gender or sexuality. It means exactly what it says—that this person is not yet sure about their identity labels and is in the process of figuring it out.

Transgender: transgender can be a standalone label or an umbrella label. People who are *binary* transgender often use the label transgender, or simply trans, to indicate that their gender is the opposite to that assigned at birth. This means if they were born with a penis and assumed male, their gender identity is actually that of a girl.

Transfeminine: also called "trans femme," is a term that can describe any transgender person whose gender is now feminine, or who expresses themselves in a feminine way. While trans femme people feel connected to femininity, they don't always identify as women. This might include demigirls, genderfluid people, and/or nonbinary people who present as feminine.

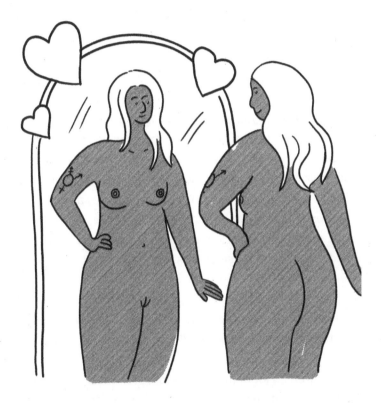

Transmasculine: also called "trans masc," is a term that can describe any transgender person whose gender is now masculine, or who expresses themselves in a masculine way. While trans masc people feel connected to masculinity, they don't always identify as men. This might include demiboys, genderfluid people, and/or nonbinary people who present as masculine.

Anonymous sex ed question box

"Is it okay to get dysphoric during sex?"

It's totally normal, and you are not alone in feeling that way. There are things you can do to reduce the feelings of dysphoria. Communication is really important always, but it is especially important when it comes to dysphoria. Let your partner know things that feel good or bad to you specifically. For example, if you are a trans man but still have breasts, it is completely fine to ask your partner not to touch your breasts during sex. Some people are not okay with removing all their clothes or may choose to keep the lights off. Some people are **trans for trans (T4T)**, meaning they are trans and interested in only dating other trans people, because they find the shared experience helps them support each other. And some find the use of toys helps them feel more in line with their gender.

"I want to buy a binder, but my parents check my search history and credit card bills."

There aren't a lot of in-person stores for chest binders right now unfortunately. Some branches of Target and Walmart, as well as local stores, sell reputable binders that you can buy with cash. You can also have a friend buy you a binder online from GC2B, Underworks, TomboyX, or another reputable company, and pay them back in cash later. Sports bras, baggy shirts, and other things that make you feel less dysphoric can also help.

If you buy a binder without your parents knowing, just be

aware that chest binders do carry some risk. If you can, you should talk to your doctor privately about using it.

"I have a few friends who use they/them pronouns, and I've been practicing a lot. I've noticed I like them for myself as well. But I am a girl, not nonbinary. Is it weird for me to use them too? Is it like when people steal things from other cultures?"

It's totally fine for you to use any pronouns that feel right to you, no matter your gender. I think of it this way—by using they/them pronouns, you are actually helping to normalize them, making it easier for nonbinary people to use them too!

Chapter 6

Sexuality
(Born This Way)

Sexuality is the part of your identity that explains who you find sexually and romantically attractive, whether or not you'd actually want to have sex with or date them. Sexual orientation is *not* a choice. It can't be influenced by what toys you play with or how you dress. It can't be changed by therapy, treatment, or peer pressure. Some people try to change their own sexuality in order to "fit in" or find acceptance, but this can cause significant damage to mental health.

Sexuality is typically determined by which gender(s) someone is attracted to and by one's own gender identity. Since a transgender woman is still a woman, if a man is attracted to a transgender woman, that would be a heterosexual attraction. A lesbian who dates a transgender woman is still a lesbian.

With our new understanding of gender, our old sexuality labels don't make as much sense. That's why we are seeing an explosion of people using new identity labels. There are *so* many labels that I am sure to miss some of them in this book.

New ones are constantly being created as our understanding of gender and sexuality evolves.

★ Asha, my teen, is a nonbinary lesbian. This confuses a lot of people, mainly because people often assume all lesbians are women. Lesbianism, however, has always included nonbinary people, since long before the term nonbinary existed. Stormé DeLarverie, a lesbian often credited with provoking the Stonewall Riots (a series of protests and riots that led to the legalization of homosexuality), would almost certainly have used the term nonbinary if it existed back then. Stormé preferred to use both she/her and he/him pronouns, which does not mean he was nonbinary, but indicates he had a very unique relationship to gender. Another lesbian, Leslie Feinberg (ze pronouns), was one of the most influential trans and nonbinary activists of hir time. Ze coined a lot of the terms we use today to describe transgender, nonbinary, and gender nonconforming experiences.

Identity labels

Here are the most common sexuality labels. People who are nonbinary often end up just choosing the label that feels most right to them based on their own unique experience of gender. For example, a nonbinary person attracted to women might use the term lesbian, straight, queer, trixic, gay, or bisexual/multisexual, amongst other possible labels. It is up to each person to decide what identity feels right to them.

Achillean: an umbrella term for *anyone* with attraction to men. This doesn't mean *exclusive* attraction—it just means that men are included in the group of people you are attracted to. This term could be used for people only attracted to men, or bisexuals who are attracted to men as well as other genders.

Androsexual: an umbrella term for *anyone* with attraction to men, penises, and/or masculinity. This doesn't mean *exclusive* attraction—it just means that men are included in the group of people you are attracted to. This term could be used for people only attracted to men, or bisexuals who are attracted to men as well as other genders.

Aromanticism: aromanticism is the romantic equivalent of asexual. Many people who are aromantic form what's known as a **queerplatonic** partnership (QPP). This may come across to some as a "best friend" relationship, but it typically has the same commitment levels as a romantic relationship while remaining platonic (friendship based). Some QPPs spend their life together, even raising families together.

Asexual: asexual people may feel little to no sexual attraction, or they may feel a type of sexual attraction that is different than the norm; for example, demisexuals only feel sexual attraction after forming an emotional connection to a person. There are a variety of identities under the asexual umbrella, and there is a spectrum of romantic and physical attraction.

Asexuals are not simply *choosing* **abstinence**. Some people who are asexual feel zero sexual attraction to anyone but may still choose to have sex because it physically feels good in their body, or for other reasons. Some asexuals may still enjoy masturbation but not enjoy sex with others. And some enjoy sex with a partner but feel zero sexual attraction until the emotional bond is formed.

Bisexual/multisexual: bisexual can be a standalone label or an umbrella label. Some people use the term multisexual to be more inclusive of nonbinary identities; however, others feel this erases decades of bisexual culture and history. As it has such a long history, I will continue to use the term bisexual for now.

Bisexuals are attracted to two or more genders. This could include men and women but could also include nonbinary genders. There are multiple microlabels that fit this category, including pansexual, omnisexual, and polysexual.

Demisexual: demisexual can be included under the asexual/greysexual umbrella or stand alone. If you separate attraction into two parts, primary attraction would be the initial attraction to someone, based on looks or obvious surface-level characteristics. Secondary attraction is attraction that happens when you know someone deeper and have an emotional connection to them. Demisexuals don't feel that primary attraction but do experience secondary attraction. So demisexuals are not simply *choosing* to wait for sex until they feel a deeper emotional connection—they literally have no sexual attraction to anyone until that happens.

♥ As a demisexual myself, I know people often assume it means that I simply don't *want* to have sex without first having a deep emotional connection. They equate asexuality with *abstinence* (choosing not to have sex). But that is not actually how it works for me. I simply feel nothing sexual without that connection...even if I wanted to. This was definitely awkward and confusing for me as a teen; I often ended up making up crushes just to fit in with my friends. Before I learned more about asexuality, I simply thought something was physically wrong with me. Understanding my sexuality is important because it helps me understand myself and find community.

Gay/vincian: gay (or the lesser known *vincian*) is any homosexual man or nonbinary person who is attracted to *only* other men and/or nonbinary people. Gay is also often used as an umbrella term for the entire queer community in terms of sexuality (except for straight transgender individuals).

Greysexual: this term contains a lot of variations of sexual attraction. Some of these might include having a low sex drive, mostly not feeling sexual attraction but sometimes feeling it, and being **aceflux** or **aroflux**, meaning that a person's identity fluctuates along the spectrum.

Gynosexual: this is an umbrella term for *anyone* with attraction to women, vaginas, and/or femininity. This doesn't mean *exclusive* attraction—it just means that women are included in the group of people you are attracted to. This term could be used for people only attracted to women, or bisexuals who are attracted to women as well as other genders.

Heterosexual ("straight"): attracted only to the opposite gender.

Homosexual ("gay"): not attracted to the opposite gender.

Lesbian: a lesbian is any homosexual woman or nonbinary person who is attracted to *only* other women and/or nonbinary people (not men).
When nonbinary people use this label, it typically means

they have some sort of relationship to womanhood or lesbianism.

Lesbianism was originally defined as WLW (women-loving women), women who are attracted to women exclusively. It is important to note that we aren't changing who is included in the lesbian community—by broadening the definition to include nonbinary people, we are simply including a group that has always been included in lesbianism. Nonbinary is a new label for a group that has always existed "behind the scenes."

Pansexual: pansexuals are attracted to people of all genders, with zero preference for gender. Gender does not factor into them being attracted to someone or not.

Polyamorous: while this is not really a sexuality or gender label, it is often included in the LGBTQIA+ community, as it is an atypical identity when it comes to relationships. Polyamorous people choose to engage in multiple romantic/sexual relationships with the consent of all people involved. Polyamorous people often reject the notion of monogamy, believing that people naturally have attraction to others and that it is healthy to explore that. One of the main "rules" of being polyamorous is that there is open and honest communication amongst all partners; polyamory is not an excuse to cheat on your partner. For this reason, polyamory is also called **ethical nonmonogamy.**

Polysexual: polysexuals are attracted to multiple genders but not all genders. This is also true of the bisexual label, but many polysexual people prefer this label because they feel that bisexual, with the prefix bi, implies attraction to two genders.

Omnisexual: omnisexuals are attracted to people of all genders, but with a preference for certain genders. Gender *does* factor into their being attracted to someone or not.

Queer: queer is both an umbrella term and an identity label by itself. Queer has a history of being used as a slur against the LGBTQIA+ community, which means not everyone is comfortable with its use. However, it has been reclaimed to the extent that many people use this term as a synonym for the entire LGBTQIA+ community—including all sexualities other than heterosexual and all genders other than cisgender.
Many people also use the term queer as their identity label, enjoying the term's ambiguity. It doesn't tell you anything about someone's specific gender or sexuality other than that they are *not* straight and/or cis. For some people, it's comforting not to define themselves further than that.

Questioning: this is typically a temporary label that people use when they are questioning their gender or sexuality. It means exactly what it says—that this person is not yet sure about their identity labels and is in the process of figuring it out.

Sapphic: an umbrella term for anyone with attraction to women other than cisgender men. This doesn't mean *exclusive* attraction—it just means that women are included in the group of people you are attracted to. This term could be used for people only attracted to women, or bisexuals who are attracted to women as well as other genders.

Preferences

Sometimes people are attracted to a group of people but have no interest in dating them. This is typically not an entire sexuality label, but simply a preference. For example, some people are bisexual with a preference for only one gender. This means that while they find both genders sexually attractive, they really only want to be with someone of a chosen gender.

There are lots of preferences we have for who we are willing to have sex with. There are also preferences we have for who we would date; this is usually a far more limited pool.

Some people have preferences for certain anatomy. This can get complicated when combined with our understanding of transgender people. For example, someone might be a straight cisgender male and only really find sex pleasurable with someone who has a vagina. This means that women with penises (for example, a trans woman who is not surgically transitioned) would not be attractive to them. They might find a transgender man with a vagina sexually attractive until they learn that the person is a man. They might decide that because the person has a vagina, they are a woman regardless of how that person identifies, and find them attractive based on that assumed womanhood.

Transphobia is the fear of, aversion to, or discrimination against transgender people.

The idea of finding someone attractive based only on their genitals is a controversial position for many reasons. Many people develop this preference out of transphobia, based on assumptions of what makes someone a man or a woman. These preferences are also often based on assumptions of what transgender people would enjoy doing with their body parts. For example, many trans women don't enjoy using their penis during sex due to dysphoria.

If someone is truly only sexually attracted to certain anatomy, not based on transphobia, there are sexuality labels that could work for that.

Androsexual: attraction to penises, masculinity, and/or men.

Gynosexual: attraction to vaginas, femininity, and/or women.

Note that these labels don't exclude all trans people. For example, if a trans woman has had surgery to now have a vagina, a gynosexual person could still be attracted to them. These labels are not meant to exclude the trans community.

Platonic vs. romantic vs. sexual attraction

Platonic attraction is the way one would feel toward a friend. While this can include really deep emotions, they are usually not *as* intertwined with your own emotions. You may miss your friend when you are not with them, but you usually do not miss them with the same urgency to be near them as you would miss a romantic partner.

Romantic attraction includes a desire for something beyond typical friendship, something that causes stronger and more intertwined emotions. People often describe romantic relationships as intimate—meaning you share more of yourself and your emotions and thoughts with someone that you are romantically involved with.

Sexual attraction is a physical attraction—the desire to create and receive pleasure through touch and action. While sexual attraction can be really strong, it is important to remember that consent is vital before each and every physical touch that involves another person.

For many people, the pool of people they are sexually attracted to matches who they would be romantically attracted to. For these people, they usually just use their sexuality label to describe both their sexual and romantic attraction. For example, most homosexual people are also homoromantic, meaning the pool of people they would want a relationship with is the same as the pool of people they would feel sexual interest in. They would likely just describe themself as gay.

If your sexuality does not match your romantic attraction, you can use the suffix "-romantic" to describe yourself. For example, the best description of myself would actually be **demisexual** and **panromantic**. This is because I can only experience sexual attraction once I form an emotional bond, but I can form that emotional bond with someone regardless of gender.

Content warning: Assault

♥ I'm bisexual but homoromantic, since I have no interest in dating men, although I'm sexually attracted to them. As a teen, I was sexually assaulted, which changed how I perceive penetrative sex. While I find that my body responds to attractive men, I also know that being intimate with them causes me painful flashbacks, and I don't want to experience those emotions. The flashbacks sometimes even cause me physical pain. I could likely heal some of this trauma through therapy, but I find relationships with women much more rewarding and enjoyable anyway.

Anonymous sex ed question box

"Is it normal as a lesbian to absolutely hate penetration? The only thing that feels good is clitoral masturbation. I cannot handle penetration even if I'm aroused. It just hurts and I don't stretch I think."

It is totally fine and normal to never want penetration. You should never feel pressured to have sex in ways that don't feel good to you. However, if you think you might just not be lubricating and stretching properly, you could try using additional lubrication or talk to your doctor about it. If you are nervous about penetration or feel negative emotions about it, your vagina may not get aroused properly.

"I'm AMAB nonbinary and only attracted to girls. I don't really like the label lesbian even though I guess I'm technically allowed to use it, but straight also doesn't feel right. I don't really want to use a term like trixic, which is designed specifically for nonbinary people attracted to women, because I don't want to always have to define it to people whenever I bring it up. What do I do?"

It's totally okay not to use any labels. For some people, labels feel more confining than they are helpful, and for others, labels are just unnecessary and not worth the effort. In your case, the options besides lesbian or straight that make the most sense are probably trixic or gynosexual, both of which are very new terms that you'd have to define to nearly everyone, which it sounds like you don't want to do. You could use the generic label "queer," or just say "I'm attracted to women," when you're introducing your sexuality to people. You can also use a label like queer for outside the LGBTQIA+ community and use a label like trixic when you're talking to other queer people who are more likely to understand what you mean.

"Is it okay if I'm a bisexual man but wouldn't ever want to date another man? I don't really want to ever come out and I feel like it'd be a lot easier to just date women and to not face that stigma."

Who you choose to date is entirely up to you and doesn't affect what your sexuality is. Sexuality is based on who you're attracted to, not who you choose to date, so as long as you're attracted to multiple genders, you can identify as bisexual. A lot of people actually do find themselves in your position, which is really sad because people should be able to date whoever they want without fear of stigma. I do hope that you find a community of people who accept you for who you are and give you the freedom to date who you want. But I also understand how you feel and would just like you to know you are not alone in feeling unsafe emotionally and/or physically to come out.

Chapter 7

LGBTQIA+ and Allies

(It's Not Just a Phase)

his chapter is mostly for those in the LGBTQIA+ community, but I encourage everyone to read it. Chances are high that you have friends or family who are queer...even if they haven't told you yet. Understanding the LGBTQIA+ community can go a long way to helping them feel comfortable around you.

LGBT, LGBTQ, LGBTQ+, LGBTQIA+...there are many shorthand ways of representing a very broad community that shares one thing in common: their gender and/or sexuality identities are in the minority and are shared by a group of people that face tremendous oppression, harassment, and discrimination. As a result, people in this community are often fiercely proud of claiming their identity, in spite of the aggressions they may face. Others are instead scared, angry, or unsure about what their identity might mean for them. And others completely refuse to acknowledge their identity, even to themselves.

I will often use the umbrella term "queer" for the entire LGBTQIA+ community. I use the term with some caution, however, as older generations may still find it hurtful, despite it being reclaimed by the LGBTQIA+ community.

What does it mean to be an ally?

An **ally** is someone who supports the people around them, usually to reach a common goal. In the case of the queer community, allyship means standing up for, listening to, and encouraging those in the LGBTQIA+ community. The common goal would be a more accepting and safe community for all.

There are many ways to show support and be a strong ally to the queer community. You can listen to people's feelings and needs, respect their name and pronouns, refer to them as their correct gender identity, ask them what compliments and/or terms they like, help them get medical advice, and do your best to create an accepting and safe space for them to be themself. This can include helping to prevent anti-LGBTQIA+ legislation.

Sometimes, the smallest and simplest gestures of support mean more than you ever imagined, especially to someone who constantly receives messages that who they are inside is "wrong" or "bad."

I'm still confused though... how do I know what I am?

If you feel confused about your gender and/or sexuality, you are not alone. It doesn't help that many of us grow up without relatable experiences in the media or seeing ourselves represented in our community. It is okay if it takes time for you to understand and accept yourself. Be patient as you separate out your true feelings from those that you have assumed because of societal expectations. It might take you years to unlearn what you spent your first decade learning.

Many people start suspecting they are transgender before they know what the word means, sometimes from as young as their toddler days. That's when people often become aware of being a boy, a girl, or not really fitting in with expectations placed on them. Kids raised in a more gender-neutral environment may realize this later, once they begin schooling.

♥ I woke up one morning to a note on my nightstand from my 10-year-old. It read:

Dear Mom,

Can you please start referring 2 me as a boy with he/him pronouns. I tried it with my friends and it makes me feel better. Sorry if that makes you sad, I've been waiting long time to tell you because I was scared and I was still trying it out.

I was shocked. This was my baby, my youngest, and I had no idea he even thought about these things. I felt extremely sad, even though I consider myself a very supportive parent and someone who is accepting of the LGBTQIA+ community. I just couldn't believe this child who wore dresses every single day and loved to sing and dance was not my daughter. I also was scared that he was making this decision so young; it felt like he was rushing into an important choice and that it might ruin the rest of his life somehow.

I kept that all to myself and processed it with other people

> and showed my child support and love. I learned that people often do understand their gender identity younger than most of us realize. But it definitely made me sadder than my experience with my other transgender child, who came out as an 8th grader, at age 13.

People begin to develop "crushes" usually around elementary school to early middle school. These usually don't involve sexual attraction until the beginning of puberty, when changes in hormones create feelings of arousal (when you are likely to start feeling more horny). But they are still crushes, with excitement, anxiety, a bit of obsession, and perhaps a handful of butterflies in the stomach.

My youngest child (they/them) has a crush on a girl who is a friend of theirs. They are in fifth grade and have recently come out as lesbian. Knowing that this may change over time, I still fully support their current understanding of their sexuality. Many kids at this age get told by their parents that they are "too young" to know if they are gay; however, if they have a "straight" crush, the same parents will often call it adorable and leave it be. This discrepancy in response is part of the reason gay kids feel so confused about their identity as they go through puberty.

Some people know their gender identity and sexuality right away. Many people take years to figure it out. It took many decades for me to realize mine. There is no timeframe that is "normal" when it comes to identity exploration. Try to be kind and accepting of yourself as you figure it out, and find supportive friends and trusted adults you can talk to. It's also perfectly okay to identify with whatever feels right and comfortable in the moment and to realize later that you didn't get it right.

♥ I started questioning if I was attracted to girls around the age of nine or ten. I wasn't really sure until I was around fourteen, so my preteen years were filled with confusion. Of course, the "Am I Gay?" online quizzes surged in popularity around that time. In hindsight, those quizzes probably made me more confused—most of them asked stereotypical questions like "Do you wear a lot of flannels?" and "Do you listen to Lady Gaga?" I didn't do either of those things at the time (though the flannels have *definitely* taken over now—I own 15!). The quizzes made me feel like I was faking my "identity crisis" to seem more quirky. I think the fact that we even have to have those sorts of quizzes reflects how heteronormative our culture is—straight people never have to take "Am I Straight?" quizzes. I think the quizzes are mostly harmless, but at the same time, young, questioning queer people shouldn't base their actual identity on them. It was frustrating that it took so long to figure out who I am, but it was helpful to consume a lot of queer media (TV shows, books, etc.) in those years to normalize the concept in my mind.

Gatekeeping

You will often come across people who want to control how these identity labels are used. This is referred to as **gatekeeping**. One example would be saying that you need to medically transition in order to be transgender, or that you can't be a lesbian if you are nonbinary.

I don't find gatekeeping to be overall helpful within the queer community. There is a lot we still don't understand when it comes to these identities, and I feel more comfortable letting people self-identify with the labels that fit them best.

I do believe gatekeeping has some purpose, such as stopping people from incorporating bisexuality into lesbianism, or from creating harmful labels like the *superstraight* movement (an extremely transphobic identity label that went around social media for a few weeks).

Coming out

"Coming out" means letting others know about your sexuality and/or gender identity. Coming out is a very personal decision, and no one should feel pressured to come out until they are ready.

I remember when I was growing up there were such elaborate coming-out scenes on TV...and those scenes always ended in families fighting around the dinner table. It made coming out seem scarier than it often needs to be.

I always recommend that people come out to just a few people first, perhaps even just one person. Someone who you believe will be supportive and who can help support and advocate for you as you come out to others. I know so many people who have come out one by one to siblings, cousins, friends, teachers, and parents and found it beneficial to slowly build up their network of support. That way, when approaching the more difficult conversations, they know that they have love and support waiting for them if they need it.

Many people join online spaces in order to come out and explore their identity anonymously. This can be really helpful if you are not ready to come out "in real life," but be cautious and make sure that the environment is safe and healthy. The internet is not renowned for being a safe space in general. The online community you join should have safety measures to minimize trolling and hate, should make you feel comfortable and safe, should not encourage adult/minor relationship building without supervision, and should take measures to protect your anonymity in case anyone comes across your device.

When you are ready to come out to your parents, it's natural to try to anticipate what they will say or do. It's often difficult to figure out exactly how your parents or guardians will respond. Some people who seem really supportive might struggle when it comes to their own kids, and some people who seem more conservative might be moved to change their views in order to better support their kids. There is no guarantee of someone's reaction, which is why it is a good idea to be prepared for any outcome. Some people come out in writing in order to allow time for the other person to process their emotions before reacting.

If you suspect your parents or guardians might not be supportive, you can give them stories to react to as a way of "sussing" them out. Tell them about a friend who came out and the reaction they got, and see what your parents say about it. Tell them about laws being passed that are pro- or anti-LGBTQIA+ and ask their opinions.

♥ When I was ready to come out, I stressed about the decision way more than I needed to. I knew my mom would be supportive, but I was scared about my dad's response, and I also just didn't want anything to change. I didn't want to be asked a million questions, or for anything about our relationship to shift. Right before I came out, a good friend decided to come out, and they kind of freaked me out. They had packed a "go" bag with all their most important things in case they got kicked out of their house. That was scary, but at the same time, that kind of helped me to relax about coming out, because I was really confident I would at least be safe. I wrote a letter with what I wanted to say, but I ended up not needing it. I was glad I was so prepared, but in the end, I decided to just tell my mom in person, and that was kind of nice. I felt brave and proud of myself. She helped me tell my dad, which was also kind of great. Not everyone was so accepting, but I'm glad I have my mom in my corner, and I love not having to hide who I am at home anymore.

If you have any worry that coming out will be physically unsafe for you, consider carefully if you are ready. Some people come out even when it is unsafe to do so because the mental health impacts of staying closeted are equally unsafe for them. Otherwise, I recommend coming out only when you know you will be physically safe and out of harm's way. Some people who are unsure make a safety plan when they come out. I know people who have packed bags containing their most important belongings (identity documents, emergency money, etc.) and kept it ready to go in case they weren't welcome back in their homes. These are extreme cases, but they happen more often than anyone would like to think.

It's important to know you are not alone. There are so many resources out there to help you, from online safe spaces to school counselors to paid therapy, doctors, and medications. There are also free resources that can be incredibly helpful.

But...why are people not always accepting?

This is a sad subject, but one that is important. There is still a lot of discrimination and harassment the LGBTQIA+

community faces; in some cases it faces violence or even death in parts of the world. I hope someday this part of my book is unbelievable to the people reading it, because I hope that people's perspectives and views can change to be more open-minded, understanding, and empathetic.

In the worst cases, being LGBTQIA+ is illegal and treated as a crime. In the best cases, the laws against the queer community have been dismantled, and people are accepting of all sexualities and genders. Most places are somewhere in the middle. In the United States, there are areas that are very progressive about LGBTQIA+ laws and relationships. And there are places still passing hurtful laws like Florida's "Don't Say Gay" law and Texas's laws banning parents from providing gender-affirming care to their kids, at the risk of losing their parental rights. But most places are somewhere in the middle. Even within progressive communities you will find people who are unaccepting, and within conservative communities you can find support.

Some people harass or bully queer youth because they simply don't understand the experience or they even feel threatened by it. I get endless comments on TikTok about there being "only two genders, girl and boy"—there are people who simply cannot or will not comprehend the idea of gender being what we decide it is as a society. My approach to online hate is to ignore it entirely—I find it is simply not worth my mental or emotional energy to respond to people who have no interest in actually learning. But when I get genuine questions, even if posed in an offensive manner, I usually will take time to educate, and once in a while I will have the rewarding experience of creating a new ally.

Some bully because they view queer youth as "easy targets," because they are part of a minority group. Some might be queer but in denial of their own identity and lash out at anything that reminds them of it. If you are facing harassment or bullying at school, please reach out for support from your teachers, administrators, or guidance counselors. If they are not supportive, find other trusted adults who will support you and help keep you safe at school. Many schools now have GSAs (gender and sexuality alliances) where you can find a community to belong to in school as well.

Other people have more institutional reasons for not accepting the LGBTQIA+ community. Many people believe their religion is opposed to being LGBTQIA+ and that it is a sin. There are remnants of hurtful laws and rules in many places, but there are also people advocating to change them. For example, the Red Cross had a rule against gay men donating blood, due to the higher rate of HIV infections. Now, they have changed the rule to allow donations from those in monogamous relationships for at least three months. They are working to further change the rule to allow individual risk assessment profiles, which is still a pilot program at the moment. I found these rules to be sad when I first came across them but also hopeful, because there are always people working together to create change.

Intersectionality

Intersectionality refers to the way social categories, such as race, class, sexuality, and gender, affect how people experience the world. These can overlap to create advantages or disadvantages, including widespread systemic discrimination. When it comes to the LGBTQIA+ community, it can be harder to also be from another group that is discriminated against at the same time. For example, if you are likely to be harassed or discriminated against for being Black, you are even more likely to face harassment as a Black transgender person.

Our identities all combine to make us who we are. We can't really achieve equal treatment without addressing all the inequities. One simple way to make change is to speak up about your experiences of being in a marginalized group, to encourage people to better understand the experience of minorities.

Anonymous sex ed question box

"I'm scared to come out, but I don't think I can live in the closet anymore either. I just feel really depressed and anxious all the time, but when I am online with other gay people I feel so much happier and accepted and understood. I honestly think my mom might kick me out. What can I do?"

First of all, I am so sorry you are in this position. I wish everyone could be themselves without fear. If you can, find trusted adults to talk to who will understand your situation and make a safe plan. There are also places online, such as the Trevor Project, that can help you do this. You can find other resources in the back of this book. Sometimes school counselors can be helpful, as can other adults in your family. Therapy, and potentially medication, can help with the depression and anxiety, and they also might help you have better communication with your mom.

Safety is the most important thing, so if you feel that is threatened, please do reach out for support from the crisis centers and hotlines.

"I think my parents are supportive so I don't know why this is so hard, but I am having a lot of trouble coming out to them. I've told my friends and even some cousins, but not my parents yet. Any advice on how to do this?"

If you feel ready to talk to your parents but are still nervous, that's totally understandable! This is a big part of your identity and sometimes people are just afraid their parents will view them differently, or they are worried about showing their identity to more and more of the world. One thing that could help is to have someone with you when you come out, perhaps a sibling, friend, or cousin, who you know is very supportive. That way, they are there for you whatever your parents' reactions are.

Another idea is to write your parents a letter and ask them to read it without you there. This gives you time to think about what you want to say and to have it ready when it is the perfect time. It also gives your parents time to process before jumping in with questions or a reaction, which can be helpful. Sometimes parents don't have the ideal reaction simply because they are so startled.

"I am AFAB nonbinary, and sometimes I just feel like a fake or imposter. I still dress the same way, usually in, like, shirts and jeans or flannels or something casual. My hair is long and I haven't really done anything to alter my appearance or voice. I am fine with how I look, I just don't feel like a girl. I guess I just want reassurance that it's okay to be nonbinary and not dysphoric or whatever."

I'm here to reassure you! You do not have to change anything about your gender expression to match your gender identity. While these two often go hand in hand, they absolutely do not have to. You don't have to experience dysphoria to be transgender. What you feel about your gender inside is what matters, and only you can know if you feel a connection to being a girl or not.

"I came out as a trans boy years ago, when I was ten. I changed my name and everything. Now that I have lived as a boy for a few years, that no longer feels right either. I didn't feel like a girl, and I don't feel like a boy. Does that make me nonbinary? I don't know why that doesn't feel right either. I want to understand my identity, but nothing really feels perfect to me."

First of all, it's completely and totally okay just to have no label. I hear you saying you want to understand your identity, but that doesn't have to mean labeling it. It might just mean coming to terms with what gender means to you specifically, how it impacts your view of yourself, how you want to express your identity, and perhaps how it relates to your sexuality.

If you do still want a label, however, then yes, nonbinary could fit. Sometimes people don't understand quite what nonbinary means—it is not one gender identity. Some people are agender, meaning they just have no gender at all. Some are bigender—both genders. Some are demiboys or demigirls, meaning they have a partial tie to one gender. Some are genderfluid, meaning their gender changes over time.

You could also use queer, or genderqueer, to describe your gender with even more ambiguity. All this really tells people is that you are not cisgender.

You could try out some of these labels and give it time to see what feels right. Some people take years or even decades to fully understand their identity.

Chapter 8

Relationships

(They Don't Exist Inside a Bubble)

Sex is sometimes just sex. But lots of times, sex is part of a bunch of other things that all together make up a relationship. And you can't have a truly healthy relationship without also having healthy communication, decision-making, conflict resolution, emotional regulation, and social-awareness skills. In a relationship, you have to manage familial, societal, and cultural expectations.

Let's start with the basics. How does someone even start a relationship? First, you have to figure out if you like someone as more than just friends. There are many intimate and long-lasting platonic friendships, so intimacy alone is not always enough to know if there is something more going on.

Perhaps you have noticed you get especially excited when you see or hear the person, or when you know you will be seeing them again soon. You might notice more about them than you do other people, and you might feel jealous of people they are close to or flirt with. You might notice physical changes when you are around them, such as your voice going higher, your face blushing, or a strong desire to touch them.

★ When I first had a crush on my husband, at age 11, I could *not* stop talking about him. He's almost all I talked about, 24/7... and somehow my friends put up with this for four years until we started dating. Every time he was near, I would get giddy and nervous, and I would blush so much. My aunt loved to ask me questions about him because I would smile but become so uncomfortable, and she enjoyed teasing me. I paid attention to every word he said, and I knew more about him than I did about probably anyone else in my life. I used to doodle my future married name and fantasize about our lives together when we were older. I guess it was obvious to everyone that I liked him long before he realized it himself.

Sometimes these feelings and thoughts include romance— wanting to be together as a couple, doing things that are not just about sex or physical touch. And sometimes they are purely sexual feelings. Either way, these feelings go beyond typical platonic (friendship) emotions and thoughts.

Asking someone out

Once you realize you have a crush, it's natural to wonder (or obsess about) whether or not they like you back. There are some signs you can look for, though there is no one way people act when they have a crush. You might notice them flirting with you, paying you extra compliments, and/ or making an extra effort to be near you. None of these are sure signs, and some people don't give off any of these signals. Really, if you want to know how they feel, the only sure way is to ask them. This can be really intimidating or downright scary, but being able to express your feelings to someone is a sign you are ready for a relationship.

So how do you get up the courage to ask someone out? If you are anxious, think of what you want to say to them ahead of time. Prepare yourself for either a positive or negative response, and make a plan for how you will handle it either way. Talk to friends if possible. Do something relaxing, like listening to music or taking a walk.

If they say they don't like you back, remember that you are every bit as amazing of a person as they are. It's no one's fault when someone doesn't like you back. It just...is. And that's okay. It takes putting yourself out there to eventually find the right person for you. Don't forget to be proud of yourself for asking them out in the first place—that takes a lot of courage! If nothing else, I'll be proud of you for going after what you want in life. Because it's true what they say: you can never succeed if you don't at least try.

Polyamory

Polyamory is the concept of dating and/or having sex with multiple people, with the consent of *all* people involved. People who are polyamorous often put a strong emphasis on communication and respect, as trust and honesty are at the core of making sure everyone is comfortable with the relationship.

Polyamory, or ethical nonmonogamy, is often considered different from an "open" relationship. Each relationship usually includes an emotional connection, not just sex. When in a polyamorous or open relationship, it is especially important to ensure all partners are engaging in safe sex, with careful attention to STD/STIs.

♥ I was first introduced to polyamory when I was in high school. My boyfriend was polyamorous, and after explaining it to me, he asked if I was open to the idea. I was, as I found the concept of not limiting myself to one partner to fulfill all my needs for all my life very freeing. At first I thought I might be jealous, and sometimes I was, but the high degree of honesty really helped me to build trust in this type of relationship. I am not still with that boyfriend, but I have remained polyamorous.

When I met my husband, I was the one who introduced him to the concept, and I was grateful that he was open to it. I never knew if I would get married someday, but here I am, married with children, in a committed relationship, with both of us open to pursue our feelings if we meet someone we want to get to know better, both emotionally and physically. We have not yet discussed this with our children, as we have decided to wait until they are older. Our relationship is so different from what society expects that we fear it would cause them confusion and perhaps insecurity or a feeling of instability while they are young.

How do I know when it is love?

Having a crush can feel *really* intense. But being in love is more than just the initial giddy and euphoric feelings. It's really hard for anyone else to tell you what love feels like. But I think love feels like something that is deeper and long lasting, something that feels like it is there to stay. It is both thrilling (my heart still leaps every time I hear my husband come home) and calming (knowing the relationship is there whenever you need it). Truly loving someone means caring that they are doing what is best for themselves, not just you. People who are in love often help each other to grow, while providing support all along the way. They listen to one another, stay in close touch with the details of each other's lives, and often do little or big things to show their love. These could be acts of kindness, loving words, comforting touches, gifts, or just making time for each other.

Ideally, loving relationships include a deep respect for one another. Your partner should help you feel good about yourself. A healthy relationship includes honesty, trust, security, kindness, equality, and strong communication.

Conflict

Every relationship has conflict. Conflict can be normal, healthy, and safe, if handled properly. Disagreements or arguments don't necessarily mean anything is wrong with your relationship. One important question to consider during times of conflict is: Does this relationship *overall* make you feel good about yourself? If the answer is yes, then honest and kind communication can usually help you resolve your conflicts together.

If you feel like you are not being respected or treated well, it is really important to listen to your instincts. They are there to protect you. In some cases, it might be a fixable issue, one that can be solved through communicating your feelings. But if you do not feel safe in your relationship, that is an unhealthy relationship. It is important to end it as quickly as you can while prioritizing your safety.

Some things that happen in unhealthy relationships include cheating, lying, controlling behaviors, and abuse. Cheating is whatever you and your partner define it as, which is why it is so important to have clear communication, limits, and boundaries. Sometimes people are not sure that what they are doing counts as "cheating." An example is hanging out with a friend you have feelings for...but not doing anything sexual with them. In this situation, think about if you are being honest with yourself and with your partner. Are you hiding things from them? Would they be upset if they found out? Do you feel guilty about it? How would you feel if they were doing the same?

Breaking up with someone can be really difficult. Sometimes people feel like they'd rather stay in a relationship than hurt the other person's feelings. But being in an unhealthy relationship will end up hurting both of you more in the long run.

When breaking up with someone, try to be as kind as possible, while still being honest about your feelings. It will hurt a lot more if you ghost the person (just stop responding to them without giving any reason), or if you break up with them over text or through a friend. If you don't feel safe breaking up with someone, ask a trusted adult for help.

If someone breaks up with you, give yourself time to heal. Broken hearts *do* heal, even if they don't feel like they will.

Allow yourself to feel your emotions—cry if you need to, talk to friends and/or family, write in a journal, exercise, listen to music for hours on end. Hopefully after some time passes, you'll start feeling like the sad emotions are less intense and start resuming your normal life routines. Remember—just because you were not the right person for your partner does not mean that anything at all is wrong with you.

Try not to lash out about your partner when your feelings are fresh and intense. You might say or do something you regret later, when thinking more rationally. It's usually not a great idea to keep hooking up with your ex after you break up...it is confusing and can make things harder down the road. It's okay to give yourself space, and it is probably important for them to have space as well.

It's also usually not a good idea to jump right into another crush or relationship quickly if you were really invested in your old relationship. Giving yourself time to heal emotionally will help you have a healthier next relationship.

Talking to your partner about sex

As I discussed in the chapter on consent, sex is not just one act, and it is important to check in frequently with your partner to make sure each touch feels good. Sexual activity should be part of your conversation when you are *not* making out, too. Talk about birth control and STIs in advance, so that you have time to see the doctor or visit a clinic if needed. Be clear about your boundaries, possible triggers, worries, and hopes. Pay attention to how your partner responds; it should be a red flag if they aren't listening carefully and thinking about your comfort and safety.

One communication trick I used to teach my students is called "I" statements. This form of communication is really clear and focuses on your emotions and feelings, something that is hard for your partner to argue with, because they are *yours*. Whatever you are feeling is valid and true for you.

An I statement looks like this:

I feel...when...I need...

An example would be:

"I feel nervous about getting an STI when we hook up. I need us both to use proper protection every time."

or

"I feel ready to do more with you, but it makes me scared when I think about maybe getting pregnant. I need us to wait until I can get on the pill, and I still need us to use condoms for extra protection from pregnancy and STIs."

Be really clear that this means *every time*. Not using condoms even one time can expose you to risk for STIs and/or pregnancy.

After you have started the conversation, be ready to really listen to their thoughts and feelings too! Active listening means listening carefully and restating what you have heard so that they know their point came across. Try not to be judgmental—if you have a kind and healthy relationship, they are likely coming from a good place, even if their words don't come out quite right.

Even though this book focuses on sex, I hope you can use

some of what you learn here to have clear, kind, and honest communication about all things in your relationship.

Asexuality and relationships

Many asexual (and/or aromantic) people find fulfilling relationships that include limited or no sexual activity (and/or romance). Not having sex does not mean your relationship is "less than" any other relationship. You just have to figure out what a fulfilling relationship looks like to you and your partner(s).

I myself am asexual and married to someone who is allosexual (someone who feels typical sexual attraction). The most important thing in any relationship is communication, and that includes talking about what it means for each of you to have a healthy and fulfilling sex life. Some people who are demisexual (like me) find that being in a relationship, or emotionally connected to someone, opens them up to have sexual feelings. Some people find they don't feel sexual feelings, but don't mind participating in sexual activity for their partner. Some asexual people have open relationships so their partner can fulfill their sexual needs. And some find their relationship completely fulfilling without sex.

Being aromantic also does not mean you need to go through life without a partner if you want one. A queerplatonic relationship is one in which people are committed to one another, sometimes even adopting a child and raising a family together, without being in a traditional romantic or sexual relationship. This friendship is quite intimate, typically having the same structure and setup as a committed romantic relationship.

Neurodivergence and sex

Neurodivergent is a relatively new term, used to describe those who differ in mental function from what is considered "typical." **Autism** is a form of neurodivergence. Being autistic means having atypical functioning on all of the following spectrums:

- social awareness (understanding social cues, tone, sarcasm, and what other people are likely thinking and/or feeling)
- sensory processing (organizing and processing sensory information from inside and outside of the body)
- repetitive behaviors (stims and routines)
- executive functioning (the mental processes that allow us to plan, pay attention, remember instructions, and handle multiple tasks)
- motor skills (gross- and fine-motor skills—large-muscle function and fine-motor functioning)
- perseverative thinking (thinking that is repetitive and continuous about negative things in the past or worries about the future)
- verbal and nonverbal communication skills (body language and expressing oneself clearly)
- information processing (the gathering, organizing, and memory of information).

There are many parts of being autistic that might impact an autistic person's experience of sex. The sensory aspects need to be managed well in order for sex to be enjoyable. Feelings of being touched could create sensory overload for some neurodivergent people, and internally the feelings of pleasure and orgasm can overwhelm the system. If you are autistic, pay attention to what helps your body to relax during and after sex. If your partner is autistic, be sure to communicate about sensory overload, and what types of touches (and how much touch) feels good. Overstimulation may also lead to trouble with emotional regulation and communication.

♥ Sex isn't on my mind at all until I've formed an emotional connection and overall friendship with my partner, and we start talking about if we want to have sex. Before having sex, I go over my sensory dos and don'ts with my partner. Not every time, because that might be awkward and repetitive and probably a turn off, but I let my partner know what I can and can't handle. Which I think should be done in every relationship, neurodivergent or not. I am usually tired for a while after, and if I have sex when I'm already socially drained or stressed, I may experience burnout or sensory overload for days.

Just like for neurotypical people, communication is a very important consideration. Autistic people often take things literally and may not understand tone, sarcasm, and/or body language. In order for consent to be informed, it is important that the partner be very clear about what they are asking for consent to do, every time. It is also important to make sure the autistic person is legally able to consent, as some people's mental functioning does not allow them to properly give legal consent.

Sometimes, sensory overload can cause an autistic person to temporarily shut down in terms of communication. If your partner is autistic, ask them how best to handle this. For some people, writing is easier than speaking when shut down. Others may just need time to process internally before they are ready to communicate externally. If you think that's the case, make sure they are safe and then give them a little space. I find communication with my autistic teens to be rather wonderful, because although it requires patience, it is extremely honest, straightforward, and loving.

Because of the potential barrier in communication skills, autistic people often suffer from various forms of abuse. Please speak up if anyone touches you in a way that feels uncomfortable, even if that person is an authority figure or tells you that it is supposed to be a secret. If you have trouble saying no, it is okay to have a physical meltdown to make your voice heard.

Societal expectations

Society offers a lot of confusing messages about sex, sexuality, and gender. So many things are considered taboo that are completely normal biologically. For example, masturbation is often considered taboo when the vast majority of people in the world do it. Attraction to the same sex is often considered wrong and immoral and in many places is illegal, but people are identifying as LGBTQIA+ more than ever before. And many places still have laws in place that hurt transgender people, despite clear evidence that validates the transgender experience.

Virginity or lack of virginity is particularly stigmatized in confusing ways. It is considered "unladylike" to desire sex to the same degree as men are expected to want it, and women who have sex at a younger age (or in some places, before marriage) are labeled with all sorts of derogatory terms. In some countries, women are even punished legally for not remaining virgins until marriage. On the other hand, a female who doesn't want to "put out" might risk being called a "prude."

Meanwhile, society often has the opposite expectation of men. Men are traditionally expected to have a strong sex drive and are forgiven more readily for being sexually active at a young age. There is a lot of pressure on males to be ready for sex almost from the start of puberty, which is often not the case. These days, that pressure is often felt by teens of all genders. Our society also expects men to have such a strong sex drive that it often ignores all types of harassment and assault from boys and men of all ages, and puts the burden of protecting themselves on the female population, rather than focusing on education and accountability of the male population.

Society stigmatizes STIs as well, though many of them are quite common. It's definitely a good idea to avoid getting an STI—but also know that if you do get one, you are certainly not alone in it.

Race, ethnicity, and culture

Each racial group, ethnicity, and culture has its own societal norms and expectations. What is expected within many South Asian communities, for example, is quite different than in many Black communities or Latin American ones. Some cultures are more deeply gendered, some are more or less open to homosexuality, some consider sex healthy and normal, and some treat it as entirely taboo. **Homophobia**, prejudice against gay people, is common in many cultures around the world. In some countries, it is even illegal to be gay.

Content warning: Rape

★ It can be difficult being an open-minded person in a relatively conservative society. Being of Indian ethnicity, I often find myself talking to people who seem judgmental of my children's nonbinary or gay identities, and sex is a topic that is completely shunned. I still remember vividly how uneducated my cousins in India were about sex, all the way into their late teens or early adulthood. I tried explaining penis-in-vagina sex to one of them, and she just could not seem to understand. I spent half an hour drawing diagrams and explaining over and over again, about the penis and erections and vaginas and lubrication. She just kept asking me, "But how does the penis get *into* the vagina?" After almost an hour of this, she finally asked in embarrassment, "How does the penis get through the pants?" I said, "OH! First you take off your clothes!" She was completely and totally mortified. She didn't know that married people ever saw each other naked. She also believed that God removed babies from the uterus when they were ready to be born. That ended up being a really funny story, but there are some truly terrible things that happen in such a repressed society. My mom told me that she knew someone who got raped in a movie theater when they were 12. They didn't know they had been raped until they got married years later and learned what sex was—only then did they understand anything about what had happened to them.

I find myself surviving this balancing act of being open-minded about sex and sexuality and still being Indian all the time. For myself, I have found it helpful to just be stubbornly self-assured and adopt the attitude that I am clearly in the right. If someone doesn't agree with me, I just accept that they are wrong in my head and move on unphased. If the opportunity presents itself, I do try to educate them, but primarily I view myself as a support for the people on the receiving end of that homophobia and transphobia. I don't know that I can change many adult Indian minds about being queer, but I do know that there are thousands of queer youth out there who are looking for acceptance and understanding from someone who looks like them.

If you are growing up queer in a conservative culture, I encourage you to find people who are supportive who are part of your same community. It is so beneficial for mental health to be accepted by people we identify closely with.

Religion

There are so many religions, and so many different interpretations of each religion's teachings, that it is near impossible to discuss religious expectations and stigmas in a neutral way. There are many people who interpret sex outside of marriage as a sin, and many who do not, all within the same religion. Similarly, there are those who interpret being LGBTQIA+ as a sin, and those who do not.

Religious trauma happens when someone breaks away from the religious rules and beliefs they have been raised with and has to come to terms with the impact of those religious beliefs. This often happens when someone becomes disillusioned with a very controlling religious lifestyle.

Many people experience religious trauma if they leave a strong religious community in order to accept their queer identity. This can often mean the loss of family support and can even mean active efforts from family and friends to invalidate their identity. Conversion camps are places where people believe they can make you straight. These places are not just ineffective, they are actively harmful.

In countries that don't have separation of church (religion) and state (government), things that are considered sins might also be considered illegal. And in countries that do have a separation of the government from religion, religious beliefs often do still dictate some of the country's laws, because of funding from religious people or groups.

If you are experiencing confusion about your identity because of your religion, I advise you to find leaders within your religion who are supportive of you. On TikTok, I come across all kinds of religious leaders who are helping people to reinterpret their religion's doctrine in a way that is more accepting of all genders and sexualities.

Anonymous sex ed question box

"I think my husband is gay and I don't know how to feel."

No one can tell you how to feel if you figure out your partner is (or might be) gay. People often focus on how they "should" feel about something, when really what matters is how they do feel. I can imagine a wide range of emotions I might have in that situation. My best answer would be to talk to your husband about it, if possible, and then decide how you feel after you understand him more fully.

"How do I find out if someone likes me for more than sexual reasons?"

My first answer's always going to be straightforward communication. While it can be awkward, working on your communication skills is so important for healthy relationships and a healthy sex life. Ask the person if the relationship is just physical for them, and let them know what you want out of the relationship. It might mean that the relationship ends, but it can prevent you from putting time into a relationship that isn't going anywhere.

You can also create situations where it is harder to be physically intimate with them and see if they are still excited to spend time together. This could include time with other people around or doing something physically or mentally engaging.

"I am transgender FTM and I don't know whether I should tell my girlfriend or not. Please help."

I'm so glad you asked this question—it is a big one. There are lots of conflicting views on when is the right time to tell someone about being transgender. You have no obligation to tell anyone you are transgender. If you plan to engage in sexual activity, be aware that it is not always safe to reveal unexpected anatomy in the "heat of the moment." There is unfortunately a known risk of an angry response when it comes to disclosing that you are trans; if you think this might be the case, have the conversation somewhere where you feel safe.

In my opinion, it is okay for people to have a preference for certain anatomy. This by itself is not necessarily transphobic.

However, a lot of times these preferences come from assumptions, which come from being uninformed or un-educated. People assume those with a penis will want to participate in penetrative sex, but someone who is a trans-gender woman with a penis might not want to do this due to dysphoria. Some might not even be able to as a result of hormone therapies. People also assume trans men who have not undergone surgery cannot perform penetrative sex, but there are many ways they can, including clitoral growth from hormones and using sex toys.

Some people choose to share this information even if they don't have to...simply because they want to share an important part of themself with their partner. That is their choice. If you are unsure about sharing your identity, it can help to think through a few key questions. How do you feel about telling them? How do you feel about not telling them? Are there things you feel they deserve to know? If it is a long-term relationship, your partner might like to know if, for example, you are unable to conceive children.

"Sex should feel good, I know...if it doesn't, how do I tell my partner?"

Yes, sex absolutely should feel good. If it doesn't, it might help to explore the reason first. Sometimes, sex might not feel good if you simply aren't ready. The nerves and anxiety can make your body not prepare properly to have sex. If you are feeling anxious about having sex, try going slower or talking to your partner about helping you relax. Sometimes sex can hurt due to a medical reason—if you think that might be the case, it is important to talk to your doctor about it. If it's just a matter of dryness in the vagina, lubrication can help.

Talking to your partner can be awkward, and you might worry about hurting their feelings (or their ego). But being honest about your own needs is part of a healthy relationship. Open the conversation by letting your partner know you have something important to discuss, and then simply be honest and straightforward about how you are feeling. Focus on what you need from them.

"I know my parents are cheating on each other and I don't know what to do."

I'm so sorry you are stuck in this position. I imagine you might feel any number of emotions—confused, sad, angry, hurt, and worried to name a few. I don't believe the burden of this should stay on your shoulders, as their child. You might opt to let them know you know, or perhaps talk to another trusted adult and ask for their support. Cheating is generally a sign of an unhealthy relationship, and whatever the outcome, it is not your responsibility to decide what to do in the situation.

"How do I tell my parents I'm not a virgin anymore?"

You do not have to tell them, though I think it is great that you want them to know. Having trusted adults in your life is really important, and I believe in open and honest communication for building strong relationships. There is no one easy way. I recommend telling them one at a time, or perhaps asking one to help you tell the other. And I recommend being direct. A simple "I'd like to tell you something and I'm afraid of your reaction, but I want you to know" should open up the conversation. Be prepared for the questions that are likely to follow—who with, why, were you ready, how do you feel, were you safe, etc.

"How do I tell my girlfriend I'm not ready for sex? I feel like less of a man because of it."

This question comes up all the time. Our society puts a lot of pressure on men to fit the stereotype of being always ready for sex. A lot of men want healthy, emotionally fulfilling relationships that focus first on the relationship building and enjoy taking the physical portion a little slower. Be honest with your girlfriend about how you feel, focusing on the things you enjoy about your relationship right now. If you believe you will be ready for sex in the future, let her know that as well. Most importantly, just remember you are not alone, and that a lot of men feel that way. The right person for you will understand and want you to do what makes you comfortable physically and emotionally.

"Do you think sex education in school will ever be improved to be more inclusive, or not?"

I certainly hope so! There are still states in America that don't require any sex education at all, which is a fact I find mindboggling. You never know...maybe this book will work its way into someone's curriculum.

A Letter from Asha

Dear Reader,

Chances are high that something in this book will be dated within a few years.

Society is always changing. Labels are always changing. The way people talk about sex, sexuality, and gender is always changing.

But I do hope that we've been able to help provide an inclusive, comprehensive sex education (to be fair, the bar is *so* low right now). If there's anything I want you to take away from the book, it's that our understanding of sex, sexuality, and gender looks nothing like it did ten years ago, which is why conversations and books like this are so important.

I hope that, eventually, this sort of inclusivity will be found in every classroom around the world. I went to an incredibly inclusive school, and still learned nothing about lesbian sex, about being nonbinary, about protection for lesbians—essentially, very little of what would actually be useful to me.

There's so much progress to be made. Even in America, there are so many anti-LGBTQIA+ laws, so much reeling back of abortion rights, so many hate crimes against queer people, and such a lack of sex positivity. I hope that, one day, someone will read this book and think about how irrelevant this whole letter is; but that day is unfortunately not in the near future.

I want everyone reading this letter to know that they are not alone, and that resources like this book are out there. Everyone deserves access to equal sex education, and everyone deserves to know how to safely navigate relationships, sex, and identity.

I wish you, reader, an incredible day. Thank you.

Asha

Acknowledgments

From Asha

I'd like to first and foremost thank everyone I've met online and in person over the past seven years of knowing I was LGBTQIA+ who's supported me. Claire, thank you for being the first friend I came out to online, at the age of 11. Arial, thank you for being the first person I came out to in person, and for being so incredibly supportive—I hope you know how much that meant to me. Everyone else I've ever come out to—my family, my friends (I can't keep listing you all because I'm definitely going to forget somebody)—you've made such a profound impact on my life, and on my ability to help write a book like this. Thank you.

Mom and Dad, thanks for always uplifting me and being my number one cheerleaders throughout life. I'm so incredibly lucky to have parents like you. There's not a lot of parents like you two out there in the world, so thank you.

To my trusted adults at school—my ninth and tenth grade English teacher, my journalism advisor, my guidance counselor, my librarian, and countless other teachers who would take up a full page if I were to list them, thank you for making my school feel like a safe space. To my classmates, thank you for, for the most part, being so incredibly accepting. I'm really lucky to have a community like that.

To my therapist, thank you for helping me become emotionally stable and mentally well enough to help write a book like this, and to help found the Normalizers. To the editors at Jessica Kingsley Publishers, thank you for giving us this opportunity and guiding us through it.

And to a million other people who have helped get me to where I am today. I love you all.

From Monica

To my husband, Nick, and my sister, Maya, who together are both my rock and my North Star. Thank you for being the most supportive, open-minded, and non-judgmental people in my life.

To my Asha, co-author of this book, co-founder of Normalizers, my first born, and my constant joy. Thank you for keeping me young enough to relate to Gen Z!

To Mars, Summer, and Leo, who light up my life, make me laugh, and support me patiently while I build a nonprofit and write late into the night. Thank you for the warm hugs and all the cuddles.

To my parents, the very best example of unconditional love I have ever seen. Thanks for encouraging me to be myself, loving me through all my mistakes, taking the monkeys off my back, and countless trips to the library to feed my voracious appetite for words as a child.

To my whole family, the Gupta Mehta Veeraraghavan clan, thanks for being my village. Anoushka, Emily, Avantika, Layla, Tommy, Bennett, Vera, Anika, and Rishi, I love you as if you were my own kids. Though I often feel lonely, I never feel alone in my heart.

To my friends, who love me through depression, illness, anxiety, and OCD tunnel vision, I love you more than I could express. Special thanks to Abril for making sex such a playful topic, to Rachel for inspiring the writer in me, to Anna for making me more open minded, to Sammy for being my lifelong best friend, and to Cassie for always believing in me.

To Parvaneh Auntie, my found family, who is a daily blessing in my life. None of this would be possible without you.

To my Normalizers family, thank you for inspiring me to make the world see you as you truly are. You deserve all of our love.

Special thanks to Seven for keeping our Discord home safe while I wrote, and to my Leader family for all the encouragement, support, assistance, and laughs. Dasani, Shawty, Hannah, Maggie, Rei, Salma, Julie, I appreciate and love each one of you.

To all of you Normalizers who shared your stories and submitted questions in our anonymous sex ed question box, thank you. This book practically wrote itself because of your willingness to be vulnerable. And to all those who offered to sort out the questions, my eternal gratitude.

To Planned Parenthood, thank you for your invaluable reference site for teens. Yours was definitely the most inclusive and comprehensive information I found online, and I fact checked myself numerous times by referencing your site.

And to the people of Jessica Kingsley Publishers, I am so grateful for this opportunity. Thanks to Andrew James for reaching out and offering us a chance to make a difference, to our editors Alex DiFrancesco and Carys Homer for making sure we were as inclusive and accurate as possible, and to everyone else who helped make this book a reality.

Glossary

Abortion: to purposely end a pregnancy, either in a clinic or by using an abortion pill.

Abstinence: choosing not to have something (in this case, sex).

Aceflux: having an identity that fluctuates along the asexual spectrum.

Achillean: an umbrella term for anyone with attraction to men; this doesn't mean exclusive attraction.

Acne: inflammation or infected glands that cause red pimples, usually on the face.

Adoption: raising someone else's biological child as your own.

AFAB or "assigned female at birth": assumed to be a girl because you are born with a vagina.

Agender: not identifying as having any gender, genderless.

AIDS (acquired immunodeficiency syndrome): the most serious stage of an HIV infection, when the virus destroys too many T cells, or CD4 cells, in your body.

Allonormativity: the idea that our culture normalizes allosexuality only, treating it as the *preferred* form of sexual attraction, or worse, as the only acceptable one.

Allosexual: someone who feels "typical" sexual attraction—the opposite of asexuality.

Ally: someone who stands up for, listens to, and encourages those in the LGBTQIA+ community, with the goal of a more accepting and safe community for all.

AMAB or "assigned male at birth": assumed to be a boy because you are born with a penis.

Anal sex: sex that typically involves using a penis or dildo in the anus.

Androsexual: an umbrella term for anyone with attraction to men, male anatomy, and/or masculinity.

Aroflux: having an identity that fluctuates along the aromantic spectrum.

Aromantic: not having traditional romantic feelings.

Asexual: not having traditional sexual feelings.

Autigender: feeling that being autistic greatly impacts your relationship to gender.

Autism: a form of neurodivergence that includes atypical functioning on all of the following spectrums: social awareness, sensory processing, repetitive behaviors, executive functioning, motor skills, perseverative thinking, verbal and nonverbal communication, and information processing.

Bigender: feeling like both boy and girl (man and woman) at the same time.

Biological sex: the physical anatomy (such as genitals), chromosomes (X and Y), and hormones (such as androgens and estrogens) that you are born with.

Birth control: medical interventions used to help prevent pregnancy.

Bisexual (see also *multisexual*): attracted to two or more genders.

Bottom: someone who prefers to "receive" during sex (penis, fingers, tongue, or sex toy); sometimes used to describe the person who prefers to be submissive.

Breasts: two soft organs that protrude out from the chest and produce milk after childbirth.

Cisgender (cis): identifying as the gender that you are assumed to be at birth.

Cisnormativity: the idea that our culture normalizes cisgender only, treating it as the *preferred* gender, or worse, as the only acceptable one.

Clitoris: a small, raised organ located at the top center of the vulva that is highly sensitive.

Compallo: being so exposed to allosexuality as the only way to be that the brain forms sexual feelings that are not natural to you.

Comphet: being so exposed to heterosexuality as the only way to be that the brain forms crushes that are not natural to your sexual orientation.

Condom: a thin rubber barrier worn on a penis or inside a vagina during sex; used as a protection from STIs as well as pregnancy.

Consent: the active permission for something to happen; when it comes to sexual activity, consent should never be assumed.

Contraceptive: prevention against pregnancy.

Deadname: someone's original name that is no longer in use, due to the distress, dysphoria, or trauma they associate with it.

Demiboy: having a partial but not complete attachment to being a boy.

Demigirl: having a partial but not complete attachment to being a girl.

Demisexual: having no primary sexual attraction (to superficial traits) but experiencing secondary sexual attraction (based on emotional connection).

Dysphoria (see also *gender dysphoria*): discomfort, distress, or unease; for trans people, this is associated with gender, bodies, and how others perceive their gender.

Edging: stopping just before orgasm and then resuming sex or masturbation later, with the goal of creating a more intense orgasm.

Ejaculation: the action of semen (containing sperm) coming out through the tip of the penis, after which the penis typically loses its erection.

Erection: the hardening of the penis, due to extra blood flow, which causes it to enlarge and point away from the body.

Ethical nonmonogamy (see also *polyamory*): choosing to engage in multiple romantic/sexual relationships with the consent of all people involved.

Euphoria (see also *gender euphoria*): a feeling of joy about one's gender expression and presentation.

Female: the biological sex of a person who is born with a uterus and vagina; *or* can be used by anyone identifying as a woman.

Foreplay: making a potential sexual partner aroused through voice, text, and/or touch.

Gatekeeping: controlling and limiting access to identity labels.

Gay (specific identity label): any homosexual man or non-binary person who is attracted to only other men and/or nonbinary people.

Gay (umbrella term): any member of the queer community in terms of sexuality (excepting for straight transgender individuals).

Gender: what our society believes it means to be a man or woman, including but not limited to expected behaviors, roles, and norms.

Gender dysphoria (see also *dysphoria*): discomfort, distress, or unease; for trans people, this is associated with gender, bodies, and how others perceive their gender.

Gender euphoria (see also *euphoria*): a feeling of joy about one's gender expression and presentation.

Gender expression: how we choose to show off our gender to the outside world, which may or may not match one's actual gender identity. This includes dress, hairstyle, makeup choices, name, pronouns, and mannerisms. It can also include medically altering physical anatomy or using hormones to match the expected sex anatomy.

Gender identity: the gender you identify with; who you feel you are inside in terms of gender.

Gender neutral (gender): a gender identity in which you use gender-neutral language and do not follow gendered expectations.

Gender neutral (general term): applicable to all genders, such as saying folks instead of ladies and gentlemen, or humankind instead of mankind.

Gender nonconforming: choosing to not dress or act like what society expects.

Genderfluid: a gender identity that changes gradually over time.

Genderqueer: a nonbinary identity that is purposefully vague; it can be used by anyone who is not cisgender.

Greysexual: variations of sexual attraction including having a low sex drive, mostly not feeling sexual attraction but sometimes feeling it, and having a fluid asexual identity.

Gynosexual: an umbrella term for anyone with attraction to women, female anatomy, and/or femininity.

Heteronormativity: the idea that our culture normalizes heterosexuality only, treating it as the *preferred* sexuality, or worse, as the only acceptable one.

Heterosexual: attraction only to the opposite gender.

HIV (human immunodeficiency virus): a virus that weakens the immune system by destroying cells that are needed to fight infection.

Homophobia: dislike or prejudice against gay people.

Homosexual: not having attraction to the opposite gender.

Hymen: a thin tissue covering the vaginal opening that is traditionally, though incorrectly, used as a marker for virginity.

Internal condom: a thin nitrile (soft plastic) barrier pouch worn inside a vagina during sex; used as protection from STIs as well as pregnancy.

Intersectionality: the way social categories, such as race, class, sexuality, and gender, create an overlapping system of discrimination or disadvantage.

Intersex: someone whose anatomy, chromosomes, and/or hormones are not aligned to one binary sex.

Lesbian: a homosexual woman or nonbinary person who is attracted to other women and/or nonbinary people (not men).

Lubricant (lube): a liquid or gel used to reduce friction and irritation during sex.

Male: the biological sex of a person who is born with a penis; *or* can be used by anyone identifying as a man.

Masturbation: any form of touching yourself to experience sexual pleasure.

Menstruation (see also *period*): when blood and other materials from the lining of the uterus leave through the vagina; typically happens monthly after puberty begins, except during pregnancy and after menopause.

Misgendering: referring to someone, especially a transgender person, using a word (usually name and/or pronoun) that doesn't correctly reflect their gender identity.

Multisexual (see also *bisexual*): attracted to two or more genders.

Neopronouns: newer pronouns used in place of he, she, or they.

Neurodivergent: a group of people who differ significantly in mental function from what is considered "typical"; most notably those who are autistic.

Nonbinary: any gender identity that does not fit one of the two "binary" genders of woman or man.

Omnisexual: attraction to people of all genders, but with a preference for certain genders.

Oral sex: sexual activity in which one partner uses their mouth to stimulate the genitals of another partner.

Orgasm: when all the intense feelings and buildup of pressure inside your body during sex or masturbation suddenly relax, releasing endorphins and pleasure.

Pansexual: attraction to people of all genders, with zero preference for gender.

Penis: an organ made mostly of erectile tissue that has a duct to ejaculate sperm and eliminate urine.

Period (see also *menstruation*): when blood and other materials from the lining of the uterus leave through the vagina; typically happens monthly after puberty begins, except during pregnancy and after menopause.

Platonic: a friendship-based relationship that is intimate and affectionate but typically not sexual or romantic in nature.

Polyamory (see also *ethical nonmonogamy*): choosing to engage in multiple romantic/sexual relationships with the consent of all people involved.

Polysexual: attraction to multiple genders but not all genders.

Premenstrual syndrome (PMS): a group of symptoms typically experienced before your period starts, including bloating, cramps, and mood swings.

Pro-choice: someone who believes that abortion decisions should be the choice of the person who is pregnant.

Pro-life: someone who believes abortion is morally wrong, due to personal, cultural, or religious reasons.

Queer (identity label): a purposefully vague identity label to indicate not being heterosexual and/or not being cisgender.

Queer (umbrella term): a reclaimed slur that many people use as a synonym for the entire LGBTQIA+ community—including all sexualities other than heterosexual and all genders other than cisgender.

Queerplatonic: a relationship in which people are intimate and fully committed to one another, sometimes even adopting a child and raising a family together, without being in a traditional romantic or sexual relationship.

Questioning: someone who is not yet sure about their identity labels and is in the process of figuring it out.

Rape: forced vaginal, anal, or oral penetration by a body part or object.

Romantic: a feeling of excitement and mystery in regard to being in love.

Sapphic: an umbrella term for *anyone* with attraction to women other than cisgender men; this doesn't mean *exclusive* attraction.

Scissoring: rubbing two vaginas together in order to orgasm.

Sex (see also *sexual intercourse*): any consensual physical touch involving two or more people that has the goal of at least one person having an orgasm through their genitals, whether or not an orgasm is actually achieved.

Sex toys: any object or device used to create sexual stimulation or enhance sexual pleasure.

Sexual abuse: sexual activity performed on someone unable to give consent.

Sexual assault: any sexual activity that is not consensual.

Sexual harassment: unwanted sexual advances that usually do not involve physical contact.

Sexual intercourse (see also *sex*): any consensual physical touch that has the goal of at least one person having an orgasm through their genitals, regardless of whether or not an orgasm is actually achieved.

STD (sexually transmitted disease): when an infection transmitted (passed) during sexual activity becomes symptomatic.

STI (sexually transmitted infection): any infection transmitted (passed) during sexual activity.

Switch: someone who enjoys being both dominant (in control/in power) and submissive (relinquishing control/power) at different times during sex.

Testicles: two oval-shaped organs that produce sperm, enclosed in the scrotum behind the penis.

Top: someone who prefers to penetrate or have the role of inserting during sex (penis, fingers, tongue, or sex toy); sometimes used to describe the person who prefers to be dominant or in control.

Toric: a sexuality in which nonbinary people are attracted to men and other nonbinary people.

Trans for trans (T4T): someone who prefers to date and/or have sex with only other transgender people because they find the shared experience important to the relationship.

Transfeminine: also called "trans femme," is a term that can describe any transgender person whose gender is now feminine, or who expresses themselves in a feminine way. While trans femme people feel connected to femininity, they don't always identify as women. This might include demigirls, genderfluid people, and/or nonbinary people who present as feminine.

Transgender (trans): someone whose gender identity does not match their assumed gender based on the sex they were assigned at birth.

Transitioning: the process of changing one's gender expression and/or sex characteristics (anatomy/hormones) to match one's gender identity.

Transmasculine: also called "trans masc," is a term that can describe any transgender person whose gender is now masculine, or who expresses themselves in a masculine way. While trans masc people feel connected to masculinity, they don't always identify as men. This might include demiboys, genderfluid people, and/or nonbinary people who present as masculine.

Transphobia: the fear of, aversion to, or discrimination against transgender people.

Trixic: a sexuality in which nonbinary people are attracted to women and other nonbinary people.

Uterus (womb): the organ in which babies are conceived and grow.

Vagina: the muscular organ that goes between the vulva (external genitals) and the uterus (internal organ where babies develop).

Verse: someone who alternates being a "top" and a "bottom" at different times during sex.

Vincian: any homosexual man or nonbinary person who is attracted to *only* other men and/or nonbinary people (synonym for gay/MLM (men-loving men)).

Virginity: the state of never having had sex.

Vulva: the external genitals of someone with a vagina.

Slang dictionary

This is a list of slang used in this book, or commonly used teenage slang for terms related to sex.

Balls: testicles.

Beating it: masturbating.

Blowjob: oral sex performed on a penis.

Blue balls: a false notion that it is harmful to leave someone's penis erect without helping them orgasm.

Boner: erection.

Boobs: breasts.

Cherry/cherries: used to describe vaginal virginity; the cherry emoji can be used to indicate breasts or a round butt, or in some cases testicles.

Clit: clitoris.

Code red: period/menstruation.

Coming out: the act of telling people that you are gay and/ or transgender.

Cum: ejaculation.

Fingering: using fingers to stimulate the clitoris/vagina.

Flickin' the bean: masturbating.

Ghosting: suddenly and abruptly ending a relationship/ friendship, cutting off all communication with no conversation about it.

Handjob: using one's hand to stimulate someone else's penis.

Horny: sexually aroused.

In the mood: sexually aroused.

Jerk off: masturbate.

Nut/nuts: when a penis ejaculates; testicles.

Pill: birth control contraceptive pill.

Protection: anything used for protection against pregnancy and/or STIs.

Pussy: vagina.

Rubbing one out: masturbating.

Squirt: the ejaculation from a vagina during orgasm.

Stiffie: erection.

Straight: heterosexual.

Tatas: breasts.

Time of the month: period/menstruation.

Tits: breasts.

Turned on: sexually aroused.

V card: virginity.

Vag: vagina.

Vajayjay: vagina.

Wanking: masturbating.

Wet: sexually aroused to the point where the vagina is well lubricated.

Wet dream: having an orgasm in one's dream and ejaculating.

Wood: erection.

Resources

United States

National Sexual Assault Hotline
1-800-656-4673
RAINN
https://online.rainn.org

Planned Parenthood
www.plannedparenthood.org

The Trevor Project
thetrevorproject.org
Text "START" to 678-678
Call 1-866-488-7386

Teen Text Hotline
Text "HOME" to 741-741

National Suicide Prevention Lifeline
1-800-273-8255

Trans Lifeline
1-877-565-8860

The National Runaway Safeline
1-800-RUNAWAY (800-786-2929)

The True Colors United (working to end homelessness)
1-212-461-4401

National AIDS Hotline
1-800-342-AIDS

U.S. National Domestic Violence Hotline
1-800-799-7233

Pride Institute (chemical dependency/mental health referrals)
1-800-547-7433 24/7
Normalizers (on-crisis LGBTQIA+ support and education) (our nonprofit!)
https://normalizers.org

UK

General Crisis Textline
Text SHOUT to 85258

Index